THE

50

BEST
RETIREMENT
COMMUNITIES
IN AMERICA

By the same authors

A Field Guide to Retirement

THE
50
BEST
RETIREMENT
COMMUNITIES
IN AMERICA

Alice and Fred Lee

St. Martin's Press
New York

Production Editor: David Stanford Burr
Design: CIRCA 86, Inc.

Library of Congress Cataloguing-in-Publication Data

Lee, Fred.
    The 50 best retirement communities in America / Fred and Alice Lee.
        p.   cm.
    ISBN 0-312-10926-1
    1. Retirement communities—United States. 2. Retirement—United States. I. Lee, Alice, 1923– . II. Title. III. Title: Fifty best retirement communities in America.
HQ1063.2.U6L45   1994
646.7'9—dc20
                                      94-6708
                                        CIP

First Edition: September 1994

10 9 8 7 6 5 4 3 2 1

Dedicated to

Our Grandson

Barret Michael Lee

"Bear"

contents

acknowledgments

Sincere thanks to:

- The hundreds of community residents who candidly talked with us about life in their retirement community.
- The community administrators and staff members for opening all the doors and discussing with us the tribulations and joys of their responsibilities.
- Our literary agent and friend, Denise Marcil.
- A real pro, our editor, Anne Savarese, and Helen Packard, our editorial assistant.
- Our family—Larry, Gary, and Becky, granddaughters Jenny and Jessie—for their support and encouragement, especially while our research was interrupted by Fred's bypass operation.

introduction

Where's the best place to retire?" We have heard that question hundreds of times at social affairs, committee meetings, casual discussions—whenever anyone becomes aware of our retirement research, they pop the question. Many times it comes from people in their thirties and forties who want to assist their parents with retirement decisions.

To our surprise, we even heard the same question from Elderhostel classmates during a one-week university program in Tucson, Arizona. These attendees were retired, but they had a continued interest in new and different retirement alternatives.

Thousands of people fifty-five and up are pondering future retirement decisions, wondering what to do, when, where, concerned about costs and about what to expect in a retirement community (RC).

In years past, retirees migrated to cities and towns in a warm climate. They settled in affordable areas where they had friends and enjoyed a quiet life of leisure. A shuffleboard game at the town courts was a diversion from sitting on the benches that were provided along the main street.

In 1960, real estate developer Del Webb started a planned RC for active adults in a cotton field north of Phoenix, Arizona. This highly successful development, known as Sun City, was the genesis of the organized retirement communities, with all their amenities, that have drastically changed the meaning of retirement.

During their fiscal year ending on June 30, 1993, Del Webb Corporation recorded 2,587 home sales orders in their Sun City West, Tucson, Las Vegas, and Palm Springs communities. Three new Del Webb adult communities are in various stages of planning and development.

Many other large corporations are now servicing this active adult retirement market. Radnor Corporation, established in 1974, is a national diversified real estate investor and development corporation with projects in seventeen states. Cooper Communities, Robson Communities, Westinghouse, Inc., and UDC Homes, Inc., are a few other companies that are developing RCs.

In the later years of retirement, people generally need additional services. The development of congregate living communities has made it possible for older retirees to live in comfortable apartments or villas with food service, complete maintenance, and activity programs. Two hotel chains, Marriott and Hyatt, have numerous communities of this type around the country; some are high-rise apartment complexes with adjacent health care. Covenant

Retirement Communities, Inc., a religious-affiliated not-for-profit organization, has thirteen life-care communities in seven states.

The facilities of the companies that we have listed above are only a small portion of the RCs that can be found throughout the country. To our knowledge there is no master listing of all RCs. If such a list existed, it would probably contain many thousands of RCs.

The aging of America, coupled with the "action attitude" of many retirees, has created a new business, and one that will greatly expand when the baby boomers hit retirement age.

The purpose of our book is to provide in-depth information about each of the 50 best RCs in America, and to answer the question, "What are RCs all about?"

We've tried to provide enough information about each RC to help you determine whether you're interested in finding out more. If any of these RCs interests you, write to the community with your questions. Ask for a current brochure, the latest copy of the community newsletter, and the current pricing structure. We have included 1993 costs in this book, but yearly price increases are common and usually take effect on the first of each year.

If you like the information you receive, schedule an appointment. Be sure to check on vacation specials or on-site accommodations for your visit. Allow three extra days to travel around the area at a leisurely pace. It's possible to sign up on-site, but we recommend a cooling-off period and a second visit before you decide.

Over the years we have traveled the country making

on-site surveys of hundreds of retirement communities and have narrowed the hundreds down to the 50 that we consider the best. Also included are fifteen that are very new, under construction, or in the planning stage, but should qualify among the best in the future.

Many factors influenced our recommendations:

Location: Accessibility to shopping, medical services, educational/cultural opportunities, houses of worship, interstate highways, and airports.

Accessibility also includes ease in getting around. We passed up many communities because of continuous heavy stop-and-go traffic on the main road. In one area we saw sixteen large billboards, each advertising a different RC—all of these (billboards and communities) in a six-and-one-half-mile stretch of highway. In addition, three shopping malls were under construction. The two-lane road was a potential parking lot.

Design of the Retirement Community: Based on the founders' original objectives, is it designed to meet these goals? Does it meet the needs of residents?

Appearance: Are the buildings and grounds attractive, in good repair, and well kept? Is it evident that residents and administrators take pride in the community?

Amenities: Are such things as exercise and sports equipment state-of-the-art? Will residents with diverse interests find opportunities to participate and feel comfortable?

Administration: What is the demeanor of those running the community? Are they candid and open with visitors? Do they encourage us to talk with representatives of the residents association? Do their comments and the material they give us match what the residents tell us?

Resident Spirit, Enthusiasm, and Loyalty: These qualities are the most important ones we look for. Do residents give us a friendly hello or share a cup of coffee with us and start a conversation with the folks at the next table? Do they smile and greet each other, as well as visitors, when they're out for a walk?

When we ask residents about their feelings, do they hesitate and make vague comments or do they honestly discuss the good points of the community as well as any areas for improvement?

Cost: Are the RCs in this book financially "good deals"? Do they represent good value? It's impossible for us to answer definitively, because value is like beauty—it's in the eye of the beholder. Likes, dislikes, personal interests, and individual preference influence the perception of good value. Therefore, all we can do is list RC costs and let the reader make the decision.

As in most purchasing or rental housing transactions, price negotiations are possible at RCs. This includes RCs known as congregate living complexes:

central buildings with apartments, dining facilities, common areas, meeting rooms, and planned activities. Many complexes have cottages or duplex housing around the perimeter, and some also have on-site health facilities. A moving allowance or a larger unit at the rental price of a smaller unit is sometimes available. It's worth asking.

From all of these criteria we will relate to you our impressions of the ambience of the community. What are its unique characteristics? What kind of people make up the community? What makes it tick?

We will also give you detailed information on climate, since this will influence your decision. Most of our data comes from the 1991 U.S. Department of Commerce National Oceanic and Atmospheric Administration, Local Climatological Data reports.

During the ten years of research for our first book, *A Field Guide to Retirement,* we accumulated more than eight hundred RC brochures. For this book we screened those and chose eighty-five as a base for our on-site survey trips. We found new RCs to survey during our travels and ruled out many by just driving through the entrance—the brochure often was a misrepresentation!

It would have been easy to choose the 50 most plush and most expensive RCs, but we wanted to write this book for middle-income through upper-middle-income retirees. Another consideration was being certain we had a reasonable distribution among RCs of various sizes and types.

During and after each trip we spent hours discussing the pros and cons of each community. We did an in-depth analysis of material received; in most cases this was thirty to forty pages of information. We also reviewed notes made on-site and, if applicable, trip reports made on previous visits. Of prime importance were the comments of administrators and residents. Eventually we reached a consensus.

Because an RC is not listed does not mean that it's unacceptable or undesirable. Suffice it to say that we had to make choices, and it was a difficult process.

retirement community terms to know

Adjacent Health Care. A congregate living community with health services on-site. May include home care, assisted living, and all levels of nursing care.

Architectural Control/Review Committee. In RCs where residents have discretion in the architectural design of their home, this committee of the residents association reviews and enforces building guidelines. In some cases it is referred to as the Deed Restriction Enforcement Committee.

Assessment. A charge determined by the RC management to defray costs of operating the community. Included are maintenance of buildings, grounds, recreation areas, and roads. Also includes such services as snow removal, police and fire protection, and the administration costs of running the community. The assessment is usually made on a monthly basis.

Assisted Living Apartment. Offers residents the independence of living in a residential setting and help with routine daily tasks such as bathing, grooming, dressing, dining, and monitoring of medication.

Build-out. After an RC is completed, the developer leaves the grounds. The residents association takes over ownership and governance of the common areas and services.

Catered Living. A marketing term for an RC; in some cases, it refers to assisted living.

Congregate Living Community. An RC that offers residents rental accommodations, meals, housekeeping, local transportation, planned activities, emergency response, and social interaction opportunities. Can vary in size from one hundred to six hundred residents.

Continuing Care Accreditation Commission. The American Association of Homes for the Aging (AAHA) sponsors this commission. The accreditation process is rigorous. It involves extensive self-study by the continuing-care RC's staff, board of directors, and residents. It also includes an on-site evaluation and review by the national commission based in Washington, D.C. The facility is measured against its stated mission and established standards of excellence in the continuing-care field. The accreditation process usually takes about one year. Accreditation is valid for five years and requires submission of yearly detailed annual reports and audited financial statements. As of February 1994, 160 communities have been accredited. A list of accredited communities can be obtained by sending a request, along with a business-size self-addressed stamped envelope, to Continuing Care Accreditation Commission, 901 E Street, N.W., Suite #500, Washington, DC 20004-2037.

Elevations. Various architectural designs of a standard house plan.

Entrance/Endowment/Founders Fee. A one-time charge at a life care/continuing care community. Refund arrangements (if any) are included in the resident contract. This is in addition to a monthly fee.

Gated Community. Perimeter fencing and a staffed or card-accessed gate at the entrance.

Home Care. Support and surveillance in a resident's apartment for those who have an acute illness or declining health, or who require care after hospitalization.

In-house Banking. In congregate living communities a local bank may have a representative on-site to handle normal banking transactions. Service varies from one morning a week to every day.

Intermediate Nursing Care. Service for residents requiring total assistance with daily living.

Life Care/Continuing Care. A congregate living community with a contractual agreement providing total care for life.

Life Line. Emergency medical call system.

Manufactured Housing. Housing that is built off-site and transported to the RC for permanent installation on a foundation. Many manufactured homes have "stick built" additions such as a garage, entrance foyer, porch, or deck.

Medical Center/Health Center/Extended Care Facility. Medically staffed complex that may house intermediate and skilled nursing care, respond to the RC's emergency call system, and provide clinic services such as blood pressure checks and inoculations.

Residents Association. Organized by residents to keep everyone informed, interact with the RC management, promote the general welfare of the RC, and in some cases coordinate all community activities.

Skilled Nursing Care. For residents requiring treatment or procedures that require a licensed technician.

Standard Lot. In an RC where homes are purchased, the quoted price includes a standard lot. Available at a higher price may be a lot that is larger, on a corner, or has a golf course, lake view, or other vista.

Xeriscape Landscape. Found in desert communities using native desert plants and stones.

THE RETIREMENT COMMUNITY LIFESTYLE

There are thousands of RCs around the country. A high percentage are in the Sun Belt, given the prevalent "run to the sun" impulse among retirees. The size of an RC varies from a virtual city of 46,000 people to a small neighborhood of 150 homes, or a combination of apartments and cottages with as few as 125 units.

Most RCs have an age restriction that varies from fifty-five to sixty-five. Except in master planned communities, anyone under nineteen years of age is not allowed to live on the premises—although grandchildren are always welcome for a visit.

The larger RCs are completely self-contained, with shopping, police and fire protection, houses of worship, medical and recreation facilities, and organized activities on the premises. Residents may purchase or, in some cases, rent their housing, and pay a monthly fee for the amenities.

At retirement, three options emerge:

1. Remain in the old homestead and develop new interests in familiar surroundings.
2. Move to "Anytown USA" to find a better climate, lower taxes, and a smaller house; to be near children and grandchildren; or to get away from past routines. Retirees who do this must prepare to be "new kids on the block" at first, before they become a part of their new community and settle into a routine.
3. Move to an RC with people of similar ages, interests, and needs. Most RCs have built-in opportunities to get acquainted. The community facilities and activities offer quick ways to gain acceptance in new surroundings and to develop new interests or build upon talents that may have lain dormant for years.

We have found that a distinct spirit emerges among residents of a vibrant retirement community. If people move to an RC and decide it isn't for them, they tend to move out. That's why we have found relatively few dissatisfied people at the RCs we've visited. A happy mood permeates successful communities, which residents refer to as "our" community.

In a vibrant RC the residents always say, "It's the people that make this a great place." Why?

Those moving to an RC have taken an action to part with the past. Everyone has left their former homes. Many also have moved away from relatives, friends, and the security of familiar churches, banks, stores, doctors, clubs, and interest groups. Their objective is to begin a new stage of life, and everyone in an RC has the same need to replace the losses that result from a lifestyle change.

Those who already have made the adjustment to an RC realize what newcomers are facing. They tend to reach out to help make the transition easier. In addition, RCs have many programs in place to make newcomers feel at home. Even after the initial welcome period, new residents can find numerous opportunities to meet people and become involved in a meaningful way.

These opportunities range from social and sports activities to hobbies, crafts, special interest groups, music and drama, educational groups, and volunteer service. It is common to find more than one hundred clubs and activities in a large RC.

However, to make a good match the individual must be willing to respond in a positive way. A standoffish attitude produces limited interaction. Living in the past, constantly reminiscing, or comparing new people to the old gang back home will make the transition more difficult.

We will assume that if you're reading this book you plan to take a positive approach to these opportunities. What will an RC be like? It can be whatever you want it to be. All residents of an RC have common goals: to do their thing; to find fun, satisfaction, and stimulation; and to live their lives to the fullest.

Each person can find a retirement community to fit whatever gives personal satisfaction, whether it's a bustling social life with the telephone always ringing off the hook and friends in and out of the house constantly, or a quiet, restful atmosphere. The advantage of living in an RC over buying or renting a place in "Anytown USA" is that the community was designed specifically to fill the needs of active mature people. The RC draws people with a desire to build anew.

Life expectancy has increased. Retirees have a quarter to a third of their life ahead of them! Couple this with the 2,500 hours that used to be spent at work and related activities and the result is OPPORTUNITY TIME!

Today's retirees are achievers, well educated, financially better off than previous generations, more adventuresome, and searching for new opportunities—hence the emergence of this very rapidly growing RC industry.

A once-in-a-lifetime opportunity presents itself when the need for earning a living has ended. When we pass from adulthood to maturity, a whole new world opens before us. Our responsibilities are fewer; time is available to pursue happiness. A person can be unique, can let the child inside loose.

Perhaps you're wondering why we are not living in an RC, since we are extolling the benefits of RC living. Because we are not retired! We have downsized to a patio home and are now in our early seventies. When the time is right (at this point, that time is unknown), we will move to a small RC with adjacent health care and build a new, exciting life as we continue our writing.

HOUSING, AMENITIES, AND COSTS

In this chapter we will cover the housing choices and amenities available in different types of retirement communities, as well as the costs involved. Specific details about each community are included in the individual write-ups.

Retirement communities generally offer one or more of the following options:

1. Purchase a home, townhouse, or condo.
2. Lease an apartment.
3. Lease an apartment with adjacent health care.
4. Lease an apartment and prepay medical expenses. (This option is referred to as life care.)

An explanation of each option follows in a question-and-answer format covering the most common concerns about RCs.

When you're considering the options, keep in mind that each person in your household should have his or her own space—ideally, a separate room for a reading chair, storage cabinet, desk or worktable, and a door that can be closed to indicate, "I'm having my own quiet time." Regardless of how much love two people have for each other, a getaway space goes a long way in keeping that love intact. Some solitude doesn't mean there's a problem—in fact, for many retirees it helps prevent problems.

1. Purchase a Home, Townhouse, or Condo

Depending on the individual RC, this option might involve having a home built to your specifications, buying a home built on speculation by the RC developer, or purchasing a previously owned home. In each case, the home may be freestanding or part of a duplex, triplex, or fourplex. Consider the number of rooms you want. Is downsizing from your current home desirable, to reduce housework? Would the same apply to the size of the yard?

If you decide to build your dream home, in a dream community, it's easy to assume the builder will conform to your dreams. Unfortunately, in the real world that's usually not the case. Disagreements between the builder and buyer are common, as anyone who has had a home built can testify. Personal expectations can also affect the experience. In the same community, for example, one couple told us they had complete trust and confidence in the developer, while another couple down the street couldn't think of a nice thing to say about him.

Q. What is the difference between an RC and a housing development?

A. The major difference is that children are not permitted to live in an RC. Usually an RC has a minimum age of fifty-five for at least one member of the household. Amenities designed for seniors, such as a swimming pool, recreation building, or fitness center, are paid for on an assessment basis, which is the same for each resident.

Q. Who owns an RC?

A. In large age-restricted communities the residents association gradually takes over from the developer the ownership and control of the common areas, including all recreational facilities, golf courses, administrative buildings, greenbelts, roads, and so on. The residents association is also responsible for maintenance and services throughout the community.

At build-out, when the last residence is built on the available land, the residents association has complete control of the community and the developer goes on to other opportunities. In essence, the residents association becomes the community government, and costs are paid through a monthly assessment.

Q. In an RC, who initiates and coordinates activities?

A. In most smaller communities a paid staff member coordinates activities. The coordinator's salary and expenses are included in the residents' monthly fee. In larger communities, the residents association initiates activities using many volunteers. Costs are included in the monthly assessment.

Q. In an RC, can I choose my own builder and sell when I want to?

A. Normally there is no choice of builder, but you can sell your house yourself.

2. Lease an Apartment (Congregate Living)

Housing arrangements of this nature can be found throughout the country. Apartment complexes for retirees often are listed in the Yellow Pages under the heading *Retirement Communities and Homes.*

These complexes vary in size and structure. Many are former hotels or apartment buildings that have been converted to senior accommodations. Costs vary with the level of accommodations, from HUD-assisted housing to plush, catered living.

In the plushest accommodations, amenities generally include weekly maid service, transportation, and three meals a day served in a common dining room. Residents might also share an indoor swimming pool, sauna, exercise room, craft room, library, a common room with conversation nooks, or a greenhouse. Many complexes have a lounge where residents gather for happy hour before dinner. Sometimes in the lounge area small individual lockers are provided for refreshment storage.

Parking is available and security is tight, with TV-monitored entrances. One high-rise community that we surveyed had a double-locked entrance monitored by a concierge.

A more modest RC of this type may have many of the same amenities, but in a more austere form. The dining room, for example, might have maple tables and chairs, with a self-service buffet instead of uniformed servers. Fewer meals would be included in the monthly fee. The rooms in individual apartments would be smaller as well.

Monthly costs reflect these differences. On the plush side, an apartment with two bedrooms, two-baths, a den, and three meals daily can cost $2,500 or more; on the modest side, a two-bedroom, one-bath apartment with one meal daily might cost $1,500 a month. Double occupancy increases the monthly charge, primarily for food costs and use of common areas.

Many people considering this option initially feel that the costs are out of line, but are surprised by a detailed analysis of their current living expenses. Maintaining a home may be costing them more than they think, and income from the sale of their house can help with the costs of the apartment.

The greatest advantage to this type of retirement living is the support system, the "extended family" that surrounds the residents. When adversity hits, residents rally around each other to a degree that isn't found in most neighborhoods.

Q. What happens if I need nursing help?

A. Many RCs have home care available at a per-use additional cost. If you require anything beyond that, however, you have to move.

Q. Can I have friends over for dinner?

A. Yes, either at a modest cost in the dining room, or by cooking in your own apartment.

Q. Where will the kids stay when they come to visit?

A. Most places provide a guest room at a reasonable cost.

3. **Lease an Apartment with Adjacent Health Care**

The only difference between this type of accommodation and the one described above in category 2 is the availability of more extensive health service. This includes home care, assisted living, and skilled nursing care.

The obvious advantage to this type of living is that residents do not have to leave the community if they require home health care. Their support system remains intact, and they receive care in familiar surroundings by medical personnel they know. For most people, this is a major advantage over entering a strange assisted-living complex or nursing home away from friends.

Q. If my spouse requires nursing care, what about the costs?

A. Payment is on a pay-as-you-use basis.

Q. Will there be outsiders in the nursing complex?

A. Yes, when space is available, but residents have first call.

Q. How many apartments are usual in this type of RC, and what would the average age be?

A. The number of apartments generally ranges between 150 and 250 apartments, and some RCs have cottages available as well. The entry age requirement is usually sixty-two to sixty-five, with an average resident age between seventy-five and eighty. The age of the community itself has a bearing on this: a newly built RC is likely to have an average resident age in the early seventies, an older RC in the late seventies.

4. Lease an Apartment and Prepay Medical Expenses (Life Care)

Communities in this category often have services and monthly fees similar to those in the previous category. An up-front payment is the major difference. It may be called the founders fee, entrance fee, endowment, or another term, but in any case it is a prepayment of anticipated future medical costs. The various options may include a refund of a portion of the entrance fee upon leaving the community. (In the event of death, the beneficiary would receive the refund.)

The financial arrangements of a life-care RC are very complicated, since they are based on actuarial tables. It is *essential* to get competent financial and legal help when considering this type of arrangement.

The advantage of this lifestyle is the peace of mind that comes with assured care for life. How much is that worth? Each person has to determine the answer to that question. Relatives or advisers may not put the same importance on this as the person concerned. Therefore, the final decision has to be made by the person considering this lifestyle.

We have talked to many residents of life-care RCs who are completely satisfied with the arrangements. With nursing care costing an average of $30,000 a year and continually increasing, residents who have received skilled nursing care for an extended time have received a good return on their entrance fee of perhaps $150,000. It's a complicated decision and should not be entered into hastily.

Q. Friends of mine had to sign over all of their assets to the community. Why?

A. Only life-care communities run by fraternal groups require this. In return, the "brothers and sisters" receive everything they need: food, lodging, medical care, clothing, plus an allowance. This type of facility makes up a very small percentage of the total number of life-care RCs.

Q. How can you be sure that your entrance fee money is safe and that the community will honor its commitment?

A. You can't be 100 percent sure. In the late 1970s and early 1980s, for example, some RCs went bankrupt. In most cases, poor management decisions caused the problems. Some of these RCs were run by religious denominations, and administrators avoided tough business decisions that residents may have opposed. As a result, everyone suffered. A careful evaluation has to be made.

three

RETIREMENT COMMUNITIES—
5,000-PLUS RESIDENTS

The granddaddy of the "super large" communities is the original Sun City started by Del Webb outside of Phoenix, Arizona, in January 1960. The development gradually grew to 46,000 residents. When all of the land on the original site was occupied, Del Webb developed Sun City West four miles away.

Most mammoth communities like Sun City are completely self-contained, with their own shopping, medical services, houses of worship, police and fire protection, sports and activity complex—everything except schools. No children are allowed. RCs that have an age restriction give notice that pursuant to the Fair Housing Amendments Act of 1988, their housing is intended for occupancy by at least one person fifty-five years or older per unit.

As we surveyed both Sun Cities in Phoenix, we noticed a difference: the original Sun City had an abundance of wheelchairs and walkers, but Sun City West had none. Logically so—the residents in the original have grown old, while the growing Sun City West is attracting the new retirees. The activity level is noticeably different. This leads us to recommend, if possible, choosing a young, growing retirement community. You and your friends can grow old together.

Thousands of seniors live in these large communities, but the lifestyle is not for everyone. What are the pros and cons?

One advantage is that whatever your interest, the community probably has a club or group with excellent facilities and equipment to suit you. If not, you can start a group and find folks to join in.

Large RCs spend millions of dollars on their recreation/meeting centers and amenities: they are well planned, have good equipment, and are kept up-to-date. Golf courses, tennis courts, bocci and shuffleboard courts, lawn bowling facilities, exercise equipment, and tracks for jogging or walking are well maintained.

At the best large RCs everything is clean and neat, with virtually no noise or crime. "We feel very secure" is a frequent comment among residents.

Among the disadvantages, some residents point out that all you ever see are old people: "It's too sterile around here," "Real life is having kids around," and "There are too many rules." And, because most large communities are built in isolated or rural locations, they aren't right for people who prefer to be near the big city.

Homes at SaddleBrooke Country Club embrace desert living in the foothills of the Santa Catalina mountains. (PHOTO BY ALINA HUSHKA)

SADDLEBROOKE COUNTRY CLUB, TUCSON, ARIZONA

An Alternate Retirement Lifestyle

After meeting the professional fitness instructor at SaddleBrooke Country Club, we overheard her counseling a resident about a personal fitness plan. A special newsletter called *Fit News* lists activities such as abdominal classes, a cycling clinic, cholesterol screenings, and a workshop on how to keep up an exercise routine while traveling. The community employs three fitness trainers.

This wasn't the first time that we had observed the emphasis retirees are putting on improving their health and well-being. SaddleBrooke is one of many RCs whose residents reject the notion of an idle retirement or the attitude that "at my age I can't do those physical things." The RC fosters development of a fitness plan and the means to implement it.

SaddleBrooke opened in 1987 in the foothills of the Santa Catalina Mountains, fourteen miles north of Tucson. It is just off Route 89, four miles from the small town of Catalina, at an elevation of 3,300 feet. The views are spectacular, especially at sunset—miles and miles of Sonoran desert, covered with cacti, that seem to lead into the mountains. Within the 120,000 square miles of desert are 1,500 varieties of plants. City living it is not, however: there is no such thing as a quick trip to a big mall. It's a trade-off—exciting natural vistas for next-door city conveniences. The decision requires careful analysis, especially if more than one person is involved.

Two phases of development are planned. Phase One consists of 1,100 acres with 1,950 homes; 1,100 homes have been sold. Phase Two calls for 1,000 acres planned with 2,200 homes to be built.

RECREATION FACILITIES	HEALTH CLUB
(25,000 sq. ft.)	(5,160 sq. ft.)
Library with fireplace	Indoor/outdoor lap pool
Café North Restaurant/Lounge	Coed weight room
Card room	Cardiovascular equipment
Pro shop	Steam rooms
Billiards	His/her lockers/showers
Multipurpose room	Aerobics
Dance floor	Massage and facial

ARTS AND CRAFTS VILLAGE (3,300 sq. ft.)	18-hole championship golf course (annual fee $1,000)
Ceramics	Six lighted tennis courts
Silversmithing	Oversized swimming pool
Multipurpose rooms	Whirlpool

SaddleBrooke Progress, the quarterly newspaper of the community, features community news and events. Following are some items included in the spring 1993 issue:

■ Edward J. Robson, chairman of SaddleBrooke and founder of Robson Communities (builder of SunLakes, SaddleBrooke, SunBird, and Pebble-Creek), announced that an application has been made with the state to purchase 750 to 800 additional acres to the west of the existing site.

■ The RV Club had planned a five-day excursion to Havasu City and Laughlin, Nevada.

■ Three hiking groups had formed to fit the abilities of all hikers.

■ Eighty women entered the annual Robson Golf Club Tournament.

■ There is a USTA Ladies Senior Tennis League. Each member must have a rating from the National Tennis Rating Program (NTRP).

■ Plans were under way for a community picnic and camping trip.

■ SaddleBrooke women hosted a tennis match with Sun Cities/Tucson.

SaddleBrooke requires at least one member of each household to be at least forty years old, and no one under nineteen years of age is permitted in permanent residence. On-site is the Golden Ranch Fire Department with paramedics. The closest hospital is in Tucson. Security is provided by members of the SaddleBrooke Patrol, made up of former police officers.

SaddleBrooke offers nine basic house models with eighty-one different elevations. Following are descriptions of three models: the least expensive, one at mid-cost, and the most expensive. All have garages, perimeter fencing, a covered patio and entry, and prices include a standard lot.

Loma (least expensive): 1,272 sq. ft.—1 bedroom, den, 2 baths, 2-car garage $99,500
Madera (mid-cost): 2,196 sq. ft.—2 master suites, 2½ baths, 2-car garage $149,500
Galleria (most expensive): 3,408 sq. ft. (two stories)—4 bedrooms, den, 3 baths, 3-car garage $180,500

Homeowners association dues are $399 annually.

One of the joys of our on-site surveys was meeting with residents. Our conversation with Bob and Hennie Westerheid was no exception. They arrived in March 1992 from California because they wanted to get away from "the California dust." After spending three months in New Mexico, they tried out the July heat in Tucson, de-

CLIMATE—1991 TEMP.(°F), PRECIP. (IN.)				OF INTEREST—
	AVG.	MAX.	MIN.	PRECIP.
JAN.	52.3	74	26	1.15
APR.	65.2	92	37	0.00
JULY	87.5	109	67	0.44
OCT.	74.0	100	36	0.73

OF INTEREST— Temperatures above 90°F prevail from May through September, with an average of 41 days at 100°F or higher. Fifty percent of annual precipitation falls between July 1 and September 15. Total precipitation in 1991 was 10.78 inches.

cided on SaddleBrooke, and have not been disappointed. Bob, an engineer who knows construction, supervised the building of their home. When it was finished he and Hennie held a thank-you cookout for the construction superintendent, interior designer, marketing personnel, and other staff members.

The Westerheids' only complaint was about noise from the construction sites of neighboring houses. To avoid the hottest part of the afternoon, the workers start pounding nails between 4:30 and 5:00 A.M. so they can quit early. Bob and Hennie spend a lot of time watching the sun coming up over the mountains!

SaddleBrooke Country Club, 64518 E. SaddleBrooke Blvd., Tucson, AZ 85737
602/825-3030   800/733-4050

SUN CITY PALM SPRINGS, BERMUDA DUNES, CALIFORNIA

Deluxe Sonoran Desert Retirement

Clowns, a petting zoo, pee-wee tennis, magic shows, a huge walk-around dinosaur, and a complete permanent children's playground in a retirement community? How could this be? Grandchildren's Day at Sun City Palm Springs (SCPS) during Easter week of 1993 was a big success. Granted, there was a marketing reason for this

The grounds of Sun City Palm Springs Retirement Community feature a pond and waterfall. (PHOTO COURTESY OF DEL WEBB'S SUN CITIES)

special day, but it did reflect a change in what retirement communities are all about.

We had lunch with SCPS resident Carol Kleban. She and her husband were the seventeenth couple to buy an SCPS home in October 1992. Carol had recently taken early retirement from a mid-level management position at IBM, and her husband was a retired technical professional.

At SCPS, Carol is becoming interested in creative crafts, her husband is "tuning up" his golf game, and both say they are enjoying square dancing. We hesitated to ask Carol's age, but felt certain she was still in her fifties. Retirees are getting younger, and the management of RCs has to think younger in order to attract and keep this new breed of retiree. It's apparent that SCPS has recognized this and taken aggressive action—their marketing plan is working. The complex opened for sales in July 1992. By mid-May of 1993, 396 homes had been sold and 260 had closed escrow.

SCPS is in the fifty-seven-mile-long Coachella Valley at the base of the Santa Rosa Mountains. The overall area known as Palm Springs is made up of nine cities with a year-round community of 232,000 permanent residents that are joined by an estimated 100,000 additional people during the winter months.

The property's southern boundary is Interstate 10, which puts the area's largest regional mall, a community college, and three major hospitals within about a fifteen-minute drive. There will be two phases of construction, each with a recreation complex, golf course, and parks.

Phase One has 37 acres set aside for commercial development. It is the first Sun Cities property to be gated and staffed by security personnel. The 1,575-acre property is three miles north to south and one mile east to west. At build-out, in seven to twelve years, the residents association will take over management of the community from the Del Webb Corporation. At that time there will be 5,800 single-family homes. Occupancy rules require at least one person in each household to be fifty-five years of age or older.

The Phase One Mountain View Recreation Center consists of a clubhouse, sports and fitness complex, tennis center, grass amphitheater for outdoor concerts, and an eighteen-hole Billy Casper signature golf course. The main clubhouse/sports complex structure has sixty-two thousand square feet of space.

The center provides a complete range of recreational, social, cultural, and educational activities. Highlights include:

8,000 sq. ft. Sierra Ballroom	The Terrace Dining Room
Senior Olympic-size indoor lap pool	Outdoor splash pool
Fitness center	Therapy spas
Fine arts studio	Billiards room
Ceramics studio	Lobby Lounge
Sewing room	Concierge
Wall Street Lounge	Board room
Club meeting rooms	Community library
Golf lounge	Big-screen TV viewing

Outdoor concert area (capacity 1,000-plus)	Playground for visiting children

There are five series of homes, with seventeen different models:

The smallest—Porcelain Terraces, The Limoge: 979 sq. ft.—1 bedroom, 1½ bath $97,500
The largest—Diamond Estates, The Marquis: 7,000 sq. ft. lot, home 2,416 sq. ft.—3 bedrooms, 2½ baths, sitting area, living/dining area, breakfast nook, utility room, covered patio, 2-car garage with cart storage $237,500

Community association fee is $1,200 per home per year.

SCPS is a state-of-the-art retirement community in an upbeat, affluent desert area. The complex is beautifully designed and manicured, and priced for different-sized pocketbooks.

Sun City Palm Springs, 78257 Rainbow Dr., Bermuda Dunes, CA 92201
619/772-5400   800/847-0754

CLIMATE—1992 TEMP.(°F)				OF INTEREST—
	AVG.	MAX.	MIN.	Annual precipitation is two to three inches, with 350 days of sunshine.
JAN.	70/43	85	29	
APR.	88/56	106	50	
JULY	106/76	115	65	
OCT.	94/64	111	56	

SUN CITY WEST, PHOENIX, ARIZONA

Fifteen Years Old and Still Growing

When Del Webb opened the first Sun City in January 1960, among the cotton fields on the outskirts of Phoenix, he offered a new way of life for retired active adults. During the first seventy-two hours 260 homes were sold. The key to Sun City's success was reasonably priced homes and a recreation center that was completely built. Buyers could see what this lifestyle offered—they didn't

Prospective residents at Sun City West can choose from eighteen different model homes, such as the Scottsdale model shown here.
(PHOTO COURTESY OF DEL WEBB'S SUN CITIES)

have to wait and wonder if the developer would keep his promises. The community eventually grew to 46,000 residents.

Eighteen years later and four miles west of the original Sun City development, an offspring was born on October 16, 1978, and logically named Sun City West (SCW).

Our acquaintance with the original Sun City goes back to 1965. On business trips to Phoenix and many visits to our Cleveland relatives who had moved to Sun City, we learned a great deal about this new retirement lifestyle and watched it mature.

In 1984 we took advantage of the one-week vacation plan at SCW while making our first survey. This was followed by an in-depth survey in 1989, and another visit at the vacation villas in 1993.

Fifteen years after opening, SCW had a population of about 21,000 living in more than 12,000 units. Upon build-out in the late 1990s the population is expected to exceed 31,000. Adults age fifty-five and over come from all fifty states and every part of the globe to enjoy their retirement years here. Average age at the time of purchasing a home is sixty-two, and within the community the average age is sixty-seven.

SCW is an unincorporated community located in Maricopa County approximately thirty-two miles west of downtown Phoenix and thirty-seven miles from Sky Harbor International Airport.

The community itself has three shopping centers with

seventy businesses, including a Safeway supermarket, Walgreen's drugstore, six restaurants, barber and beauty salons, clothing stores, gift shops, and more. There are ten financial institutions. In addition, there are many small shopping centers in the area surrounding the main entrance. Bell Road is the principal artery to I-17, which connects to I-10. Eight miles east on Bell Road is Arrowhead Town Center, a large regional shopping mall that opened in October 1993.

SCW's majestic library, highlighted by its clock tower, has forty thousand volumes. Twelve religious organizations meet in their own houses of worship or in community rooms, and most major faiths are represented. On-site is the not-for-profit, multistory, 203-bed Del E. Webb Hospital, a 120-bed extended-care facility, and a 196-unit catered-living retirement center. There is also a funeral chapel.

Set apart is the model home community, which features eighteen fully furnished homes and a design and color center. Prospective residents can wander on their own with a price sheet that lists descriptions, sizes, and costs of sixty-three different housing options. All home prices include a standard homesite, landscaping, and irrigation in the front yard.

The Casitas (three styles) are the least expensive dwellings, ranging from $73,700 (1,102 sq. ft.) to $81,800 (1,330 sq. ft.).

The most expensive are the two styles of Estate

homes. These require a premium oversized lot and sell for $208,600 (2,903 sq. ft.).

The most popular homes are the Premieres (twenty-three styles), $95,700 (1,295 sq. ft.) to $157,200 (2,705 sq. ft.). Del Webb Company builds all the homes. The mandatory Property Owners and Residents Association dues are $110 a year per person.

The $14 million R. H. Johnson Recreation Center was the first building completed at Sun City West. It covers forty acres and includes an Olympic-size pool; a ballroom; bowling lanes; billiard tables; craft studios; a miniature golf course; a one-quarter-mile running track; fifteen tennis courts; handball, racquetball, and squash courts; card-playing rooms; meeting rooms; and a 1,200-seat social hall for meetings, dances, and other activities. There is also a playground for the grandchildren.

Sundome Center, a 7,169-seat single-level theater, owned by Arizona State University, adjoins the recreation center. It provides seating for 78 wheelchairs, and has a dance floor of 5,700 square feet (space for 500 couples). The parking lot has space for 3,166 vehicles. Recent summer musicals included performances by Harry Belafonte, Tommy Tune, and Dolly Parton.

As new areas developed, additional recreation centers were built. Beardsley Park, a second center, features a large indoor-outdoor pool allowing comfortable year-round use; a spa; craft rooms; and a park complete with bandstand, cabañas, and barbecue pits. The Fred Kuentz Recreation Center has a three hundred-seat theater, craft rooms, a heated outdoor pool, and a softball field. A fourth multimillion-dollar recreation center is scheduled to open in April 1994.

SCW has eighty-nine registered clubs, plus various other activities that take the activity list to well over one hundred. Volunteering is coordinated through a Volunteer Bureau that services both Sun Cities. Since its inception in 1982, the bureau has placed more than 3,500 volunteers throughout the Sun Cities and in many activities outside the communities, including a food bank and assistance programs in El Mirage, a migrant farm worker's community.

In one of the auditoriums, while a tap dancing line was practicing on stage, we talked with Beverley Bradshaw, president of the Rhythm Tappers. A membership club of 175, including ten men, the Tappers range in age from fifty to eighty-three, with an average of sixty-eight. Although very few members have ever danced professionally, the group has performed throughout the United States and in Japan and Russia. They stage a major spring and winter show at SCW, compete in the Seniors Division of the National Competition of Headliners in Las Vegas, and entertain at nursing homes, clubs, and other groups. Other active SCW groups include a military-style drill team and a jazz drill team that participates in parades.

Beverley moved to SCW from Houston twelve years ago. We didn't have to ask her if she liked her retirement—her enthusiasm was obvious! She had what we call meaningful purpose, the feeling that makes it worthwhile to get up in the morning and get going.

Some residents join the PRIDES (Proud Residents

CLIMATE—1991 TEMP. (°F), PRECIP. (IN.)				OF INTEREST—
	AVG.	MAX.	MIN.	PRECIP.
JAN.	55.9	76	36	0.63
APR.	72.2	97	49	0.00
JULY	95.1	112	72	0.14
OCT.	80.2	105	46	1.16

OF INTEREST— Elevation is 1,100 feet in the Sonoran Desert. Total precipitation in 1991 was 8.35 inches. Thunderstorms are common in July and August. From 1962 through 1991, the most measurable snowfall was 0.4 inches in December 1990. The most precipitation was 15.28 inches in 1978.

Independently Donating Essential Service), who weekly prowl the streets with garbage bags, rakes, and tree trimmers to keep their community clean and neat. Members of the volunteer Sheriff's Posse patrol the streets as the eyes and ears of the Maricopa County Sheriff's Office, twenty-four hours a day, seven days a week. They have helped achieve and maintain one of the lowest crime rates per capita in the country.

SCW's recreation centers are owned, debt-free, by the residents association. At build-out the association also will own all of the common grounds. Residents have continual involvement in the operation of the community, so that the eventual transition of ownership can be made most effectively.

SCW is utopia for some, tolerable for others. Some residents, for example, were not happy when the common areas went smoke-free in 1993. This RC is large enough, however, to offer a wide range of opportunities for a satisfying and comfortable retirement.

Sun City West, 13001 Meeker Blvd., Sun City West, AZ 85375
602/957-2270   800/528-2604

SUN LAKES COUNTRY CLUB, BANNING, CALIFORNIA

What a Difference 2,350 Feet Makes

Driving west on I-10 in the San Gorgonio Pass, flanked by the San Bernardino Mountains to the north and the San Jacinto Mountains to the south, we headed into a strong wind with accompanying dust. Thousands of windmill generators on both sides of the road were rotating furiously. Although they made an unattractive first impression, the wind and the elevation of 2,350 feet gave us welcome relief from the heat of the low desert.

When we commented on this to residents Dick and Pat Webber, Dick told us that during the winter months the strong winds make temperatures in the thirties and forties feel even colder. Once or twice a year a blanket of snow will appear in the morning.

The Webbers were manning an information table in the recreation center, and talked with us later in the library. They have been Sun Lakes residents for four-and-a-half years, and Dick is one of the thirteen district representatives in the homeowners association.

According to the Webbers, a small community like this (970 acres, 1,635 homes sold as of 1993) is like a big family, with a lot of spontaneous socializing. After a loss, the survivor gets back into the mainstream very rapidly.

Because the residents know they will eventually own and manage the entire complex, most are heavily involved not only in clubs and activities, but also in volunteer work for the community such as manning the information desk, keeping the community neat and clean, and making sure that new people have every opportunity to become an integral part of the family.

Whenever a group of people is involved, there will be some differences of opinion. Sun Lakes residents say they make an effort to work out problems because everyone has made an investment and knows it's "our community, our lifestyle, so let's make it the best there is."

Sun Lakes Country Club, a guard-gated community for adults fifty-five and over, was opened in 1987 by the Presley Companies. This corporation has built more than 37,000 homes in California, Arizona, Illinois, and New Mexico. Build-out at Sun Lakes is expected just before the turn of the century.

The site has an eighteen-hole, par-seventy-two golf course and driving range and a Mediterranean-style club-house/recreation center with tennis courts, a pool, spa, billiards, craft center, fitness center, grand ballroom, Sand Wedge Café, and Masters Lounge. There are twenty-four clubs and activities listed in the residents' handbook. The square dancing club has a membership of ninety-four couples, and the softball team competes in a ten-team intercity league.

The average age is sixty-four. Most residents come from within California, and 95 percent live at Sun Lakes year-round. Sun Lakes is forty-five minutes from snow skiing, thirty minutes from Palm Springs, and about an hour (non-rush hour) from Los Angeles. The hospital in Banning is one mile from the RC. Outside the gate of the community is a shopping center with a Kmart, Albertson's supermarket, gas station, drugstore, dentist/medical group, bank, restaurant, postal annex, and specialty shops.

The development of a retirement center at Sun Lakes with an executive golf course, congregate living, continuing care, and small homes is under consideration. This would be separate from the existing community.

Every home purchaser pays a one-time country club initiation fee of $950 per lot. The monthly fee to the association is $93, which includes $20 for social membership dues.

Sun Lakes has fourteen different house styles. Each has a two-car garage. Costs reflect building on a standard lot; lots adjoining the golf course cost an additional $25,000 to $45,000.

VILLA SERIES Duplex, 3 models:

Residents in these homes pay a subassociation fee of $110 per month, which covers outside maintenance of the structure, landscape maintenance, building insurance, and upkeep of the villa pool/spa for duplex owners' use only.

Pebble Beach (midsize): 1,253 sq. ft.—2 bedrooms, 2 baths $120,990

LEGEND SERIES, 3 models
Sunningdale (midsize): 1,469 sq. ft.—2 bedrooms, 2 baths, plus den $130,990

RESORT SERIES, 4 models
Riviera (midsize): 1,550 sq. ft.—2 bedrooms, 2 baths, retreat or bedroom $149,990

CLASSIC SERIES, 4 models
Eagleridge (smallest): 1,895 sq. ft.—3 bedrooms, 2 baths $181,000
Augusta (largest): 2,629 sq. ft.—3 bedrooms, loft, 2½ baths $216,000

The snowcapped mountains, man-made lakes and rippling falls, palms and plantings, curving roads, and excellent maintenance is all impressive. But the message on the buttons worn by many of the residents tells the real story: **"It's the People."**

CLIMATE—1992 TEMP. (°F)			OF INTEREST—
AVG.	MAX.	MIN.	Sun Lakes has cooler temperatures than the Palm Springs area, so be prepared for high winds, occasional snow, and the need for winter clothing.
JAN. 64/41	77	28	
APR. 74/45	91	34	
JULY 93/60	104	50	
OCT. 84/53	102	45	

Sun Lakes Country Club, 850 South Country Club Drive, Banning, CA 92220
909/845-2123   800/368-8887

SUN LAKES COUNTRY CLUBS, SUN LAKES, ARIZONA

First Robson Adult Community

The Dancing Grannies of Sun Lakes have attained national acclaim. They won a first-place award at the Fiesta Bowl Parade, have marched in the Macy's Thanksgiving Day Parade, and perform around the country and on cruise ships. Residents Helga and Jerry Morris spent an hour telling us about their life at Sun Lakes and answering questions. Helga is a Dancing Granny and part of the nine-person core group of aerobic dancers. When preparing for a show she practices four hours a day. Jerry is a retired colonel who met Helga when he commanded a military base in Germany years ago.

This couple is enthusiastic about Sun Lakes, saying that the facilities are excellent and the people friendly. They emphasized the value of the block parties, when streets are closed and neighbors get together. Helga and Jerry participate in the Preferred Guest Program as host residents and have dinner with prospective buyers on the first evening of their four-day, three-night stay.

In 1972 Robson Communities acquired 2,560 acres of

The Palo Verde golf course is one of five courses available to residents of Sun Lakes Country Club.   (PHOTO BY STEVE CUTTER)

land in the Chandler area, twenty-three miles southeast of Phoenix. Originally a manufactured housing development, it changed to single-family homes that are built on-site. Robson purchased additional acreage in mid-1993 for a total of 3,400 acres, on which 5,865 homes have been built. This is a community for active adults. One member of each household must be at least forty years old, with no one in permanent residence under the age of nineteen.

Build-out is expected in fifteen to twenty years, with a total of about 10,000 homes.

Sun Lakes is located in the southernmost part of Maricopa County, just across the line from Pinal County. I-10 is three miles to the west, and the North Chandler Regional Hospital is fifteen minutes to the north.

Average age of the residents is approximately sixty, and 80 percent are from out of state. The top two states of origin are California (about 25 percent) and Washington (about 6 percent). Close to 8 percent of the residents are from Canada.

Property is developed in phases, each centered on a country club. Ironwood Country Club, now under way, features a 5,500-yard par-sixty-seven golf course designed for the intermediate golfer. One resident described it as "something between a championship course and an executive course." Of the 101 total golf course acres, only 5 acres will retain the desert landscape. The rest will be covered with grass.

One of the four golf course lakes is directly north of the five thousand-square-foot clubhouse, which has a three thousand-square-foot covered patio. A swimming pool, spa, and putting green are nearby. The clubhouse is expected to be completed in 1994; the golf course already is playable. Residents are expected to move in by early 1994.

The three other golf courses are Cottonwood, Palo Verde, and Oakwood. Additional recreational facilities include nine lighted tennis courts, six heated pools, indoor racquetball courts, men's and women's exercise rooms, whirlpools, saunas, and a softball field. There is a seven thousand-square-foot multipurpose auditorium, with separate rooms for arts and crafts, ceramics, painting, lapidary, educational classes, billiards, cards, dance studio, and library.

Community services include a safety patrol, mini storage, RV storage, two county fire stations with ambulance and paramedics, vacation watch, a county library, and houses of worship.

Commercial facilities include a medical center, two pharmacies, a supermarket, bank, hardware store, full-service garage and tire store, video store, florist, veterinarian, beauty/barber shop, and post office.

The price guide lists fifteen different model homes with three elevations for each model. All houses include a two-car garage, perimeter masonry wall, fully developed standard homesite, covered patio, and villa tile roof.

Representative homes and prices:

Pinnacle: 1,060 sq. ft.—one bedroom, den, two baths
$89,950

Monterey: 1,674 sq. ft.—two bedrooms, family room, two baths
$109,150

Hermosa: 2,000 sq. ft.—two bedrooms, family room, two baths
$136,900

Borgata: 2,620 sq. ft.—two bedrooms, den, two-and-one-half baths
$161,900

Monthly homeowners and association dues are $50 per household. The residents association will take over full control of the entire complex at build-out.

Sun Lakes Splash is a monthly ninety-six-page tabloid paper sent to all households in the community. Each issue has many advertisements, but it's also full of news about what's going on in Sun Lakes. For example, one 1993 issue reported that the Chandler Regional Hospital was purchasing land within the complex for future development of a health center; it also reported news about the homeowners association, Harmonairs (Barbershop Chorus), little theater group, Kiwanis Club, RVers, VFW-AUX, writer's workshop, dance club, American Legion Post 55, and a list of all meetings scheduled for the month. Residents are kept fully informed.

The Phoenix area is in the Sonoran Desert, the lowest and hottest of the four deserts on the North American continent. We asked Jerry Morris whether residents minded the intense heat of the summer months. He said it takes about a year to adjust to the climate, and the pool

CLIMATE—1991 TEMP. (°F), PRECIP. (IN.)

	AVG.	MAX.	MIN.	PRECIP.
JAN.	55.9	76	36	0.63
APR.	72.2	97	49	0.00
JULY	95.1	112	72	0.14
OCT.	80.2	105	46	1.16

OF INTEREST—
Elevation is 1,100 feet in the Sonoran Desert. Total precipitation in 1991 was 8.35 inches. Thunderstorms peak in July and August. From 1962 to 1991, the highest measurable snowfall was 0.4 inches in December 1990. The most precipitation was 15.23 inches in 1978.

becomes the central meeting place for "the gang" during the summer. In these months, activities start at 5:00 A.M., and residents stay indoors between noon and 4:00 P.M., the hottest part of the day. According to Jerry, adjusting your schedule around the heat makes it tolerable.

Southwestern living at Sun Lakes includes stucco houses, tile roofs, Xeriscape landscaping (desert plants, colored stones), spacious high-ceiling rooms, pastel colors, and informality. Adjustments are required by former cold-climate residents who make the "run to the sun."

Sun Lakes Country Clubs, 25025 E. J. Robson Blvd., Sun Lakes, AZ 85248
602/895-9600   800/321-8643

WESTBROOK VILLAGE, PEORIA, ARIZONA

Divided, but United

"I've probably sold more homes than some of the salesmen," said Westbrook Village resident George Bure. Throughout our conversation, his enthusiasm came through loud and clear.

George said he officially retired at age fifty-five in 1985—but not really! Instead, he went from selling women's shoes to designing computer graphics. A Westbrook Village resident for three years, he still does some graphics business, but making toy soldiers is his main interest. He cast his first soldier as a kid and has continued ever since. His claim to fame is a set of soldiers he gave to President Reagan that is now on display in the Reagan Library in California.

George said he is "not a retiree sitting around waiting to die," which is undoubtedly an understatement. His outlook on life is contagious—and, appropriately, he lives on West Utopia Road!

The adult community of Westbrook Village is located twenty-seven miles northwest of downtown Phoenix and thirty-two miles from Sky Harbor International Airport. In May 1993, 2,300 homes had been built, with 1,400 to go before build-out in another four to five years. The community is being built in two phases of 640 acres each, with 91st Street separating the phases.

The property includes two membership country clubs not included in the yearly residents association fee of $306 per household. Westbrook Village Country Club, in Phase One, and Vistas Club at Westbrook Village, in Phase Two, each has an eighteen-hole championship course and clubhouse. The fees cover the operation of the two recreation centers, one in each phase, and maintenance of the common areas. At build-out, when the residents association takes control of the community, it will have the first option to buy the clubs.

Within the community there are two seventy-five-foot pools, two spas, and six lighted tennis courts, including a stadium court. There is an aerobics room, weight room, and a cardiovascular workout room. Crafts include two art and ceramics studios, a lapidary shop, wood shop, stained glass and needle arts rooms. Each recreation center has a large auditorium with stage and numerous meeting rooms.

The fitness and activity guide lists twelve organized card and game groups, light dance and exercise groups including Dancercise, Jazzercise, tap dance, and a dawn walk/sunset stride club, ten sport groups, and ten state groups, plus a Canadian club. Many volunteer and educational programs are active as well, and special events include an arts and crafts fair, yearly flea markets, and holiday celebrations.

UDC Homes has divided Westbrook Village into eighteen neighborhoods. For example, Vista Pinnacle is a gated community of fifty-seven premium lots bordered by the golf course in Phase Two. An expensive series of homes has been designed for the premium lots.

Two residents are elected from each neighborhood to serve on the board of the residents association. One member of each household must be forty or older, and the average age is fifty-seven. Arrowhead Hospital is ten minutes away, and the Peoria Police and Fire Department with paramedics has a four-minute response time.

Two miles away, Arrowhead Town Center Mall—92 acres, with 102 stores—opened in October 1993. Golf carts can be driven to the mall via back roads.

There are five series of homes, all with a two-car garage; prices for a standard lot are as follows:

CASITAS—4 models (attached)
Barbados (smallest): 1,368 sq. ft.—2 bedrooms, 2 baths
$98,900

RANCH—5 models
Celeste (midsize): 1,533 sq. ft.—dual master suites, 2
baths $105,500

CLASSIC—8 models
Camelback (midsize): 1,842 sq. ft.—2 bedrooms, 2 baths,
den, Arizona room (family room) $125,900

EXECUTIVE—5 models
Santa Barbara (midsize): 2,206 sq. ft.—2 bedrooms, 2
baths, hobby room, Arizona room $147,900

ESTATE—8 models (5 have 3-car garages)
Barrington (midsize): 2,431 sq. ft.—2 bedrooms/den, 2
baths, Arizona room, 3-car garage $185,900

Before we left Westbrook we stopped at the country club
for a cold drink. A resident named Jan Palmer came over
and asked if we were new in the community. We explained our reason for being there and had a fine conversation. Jan, a former hospital volunteer, said that when
her husband died four years after moving with her to
Westbrook, the community rallied around her and helped
her through the adjustment. She said she is always included in activities and still feels very much a part of the
group.
     Over the years we continue to marvel at the friend-
liness of RC residents. Westbrook village was no exception. The only reason that we can come up with is that
they are happy in their environment and want others to
feel the same way.

CLIMATE—1991 TEMP. (°F), PRECIP. (IN.)				OF INTEREST—
	AVG.	MAX.	MIN.	PRECIP.
JAN.	55.9	76	36	0.63
APR.	72.2	97	49	0.00
JULY	95.1	112	72	0.14
OCT.	80.2	105	46	1.16

OF INTEREST— Elevation is 1,100 feet in the Sonoran Desert. Total precipitation in 1991 was 8.35 inches. Thunderstorms peak in July and August. From 1962 to 1991, the highest measurable snowfall was 0.4 inches in December 1990. The most precipitation was 15.23 inches in 1978.

Westbrook Village, 18827 Country Club Parkway, Peoria, AZ 85382

602/933-0181   800/892-2838

FUTURE: DEL WEBB

Del Webb Corporation has announced plans for three new communities.

Sun City, Georgetown, Texas

Sun City has options on approximately four thousand acres near Georgetown, Texas. If this progresses as planned, they could break ground in 1995.

Sun City, Hilton Head, South Carolina

A June 1993 press release announced that 5,100 acres of land had been optioned ten miles northwest of Hilton Head Island. Phillip J. Dion, Del Webb chairman and CEO, said, "We have studied various regions along the east coast and believe this location offers one of the best combinations of climate, natural beauty, shopping, medical facilities and access to historic and recreational attractions." Update as of March 1994: Sun City has established an office at Hilton Head. They have received all approvals and expect possible ground breaking in May 1994.

Sun City, Roseville, California

The corporation's press release about its fourth-quarter financial results, dated July 26, 1993, said, "We are continuing the entitlement process in Roseville, California, for a planned active adult community in this beautiful town outside Sacramento." Ground was broken at this site in February 1994.

For information about these communities, contact: Del Webb Corporation, Public & Community Relations, 2231 E. Camelback Rd., P.O. Box 29040, Phoenix, AZ 85038 602/808-8000

FUTURE: PEBBLE CREEK

Pebble Creek Golf Resort, Goodyear, Arizona

At build-out, too far in the future to predict, this 2,200-acre adult community will have 5,500 homes. November 1992 was the official opening of the 760-acre Phase One. Nine holes of an eighteen-hole golf course were available for play in May 1993.

Construction of the thirty thousand square-foot clubhouse began in January 1993. Called Eagles Nest, it will combine a golf course and pro shop with an activity center for the community. Floor plans include a staffed reception area and large lobby with fireplace, auditorium with stage, dining and banquet room, lounge, meeting room, library (also with fireplace), post office, weight room, aerobic room, pool and spa, his/her steam and massage rooms, lap pool, and spa. Tennis courts will be adjacent to the clubhouse and there will be a separate arts and crafts center.

There are three series of homes, and ten model homes have been built. Rough price estimates are as follows:

Casita Series: 1,110 to 1,650 sq. ft. $80,000–100,000
Premiere Series: 1,200 to 2,120 sq. ft. $90,000–120,000
Luxury Series: 1,800 to 3,400 sq. ft. $130,000–170,000

The monthly homeowners and association fee is $50 per household. Pebble Creek is about eighteen miles west of downtown Phoenix. I-10 and shopping are within a five-minute drive.

We had an interesting and unusual conversation with Jim and Lorraine Jones, who were anxiously awaiting the completion of their home. As they planned their retirement, they surveyed the Sun Belt states and decided on the Phoenix area. They became enthusiastic about the layout, house design, and Greater Phoenix location of Pebble Creek.

All smiles, they told us they also liked this area because "we're fresh fruit and vegetable fanatics." On Indian School Road near the community are 148 acres of truck farms where visitors can "pick and pull" their choice of produce. An added bonus is that there are two harvests a year: May/June and again in September. This feature, along with the Joneses' goal to play the one hundred best golf courses around the country, promises to bring them retirement satisfaction.

Pebble Creek Golf Club should develop into a highly desirable adult community—even for those who prefer meat and potatoes.

Pebble Creek Golf Resort, 3639 Clubhouse Dr., Goodyear, AZ 85338
800/795-4663

RETIREMENT COMMUNITIES— 1,000 TO 5,000 RESIDENTS

Communities in this classification are scaled-down versions of the largest communities. They have all the usual amenities, including a first-class recreation center.

Many of the large communities covered in the previous chapter started out with a potential of perhaps 1,500 homes. As build-out approached, if there was adjacent land available, the developer purchased it and added one or more new sections.

Most likely this will happen with some of the medium-sized communities included in this chapter.

HERITAGE VILLAGE, SOUTHBURY, CONNECTICUT

Maturity

In the early 1960s Henry Papparazzo bought two large farms and the former estate of entertainer Victor Borge.

Heritage Village homes and the library border one of the community's many attractive ponds. (PHOTO BY RICHARD B. HOWARD)

His dream was to build an age-restricted fifty-five-plus village on these one thousand acres of rolling countryside in the southwest part of Connecticut.

Construction started in 1967, and by mid-1976 all of the 2,580 condominium units, including the model homes, had been sold. The village is located in the small town of Southbury along I-84, ten miles southwest of Waterbury, fifteen miles northeast of Danbury, twenty-five miles north of Long Island Sound, and seventy-five miles from New York City.

A map of the village looks like a gigantic jigsaw puzzle. Every main road curves; some end with a turnaround, others form circles, and some join with other curving roads. Small lanes branch off these roads, with clusters of eight to fourteen one- and two-story units at the end of each lane. This community layout conforms to the terrain and blends in with the pine, fir, and other trees that have been left in their natural state. All utilities are underground and fourteen ponds and lakes dot the landscape. A rustic natural look prevails. The units are placed to meld with the terrain and form mini-neighborhoods separated by hills, ponds, and trees. The exterior of the buildings is cedar stained in New England colors of natural brown, green, and gray.

The Pomperaug River runs along the eastern border of the property. Housing extends from the village green and shopping area that is centered on the eastern border. A western sector is separated from the rest of the village by a large wildlife and game reserve.

Original buildings from the Borge estate are used for community activities. A turn-of-the-century house known as the Meeting House contains a TV, music and card rooms, a magazine exchange, and the village administrative offices. Ethan Allen Cottage houses the library; the old stable is used for arts and crafts; and Winship Barn houses the woodworking and metal crafts shop. The Woman's Club and Men's Club have separate buildings.

The activity building has a pool (there are three others throughout the community), gymnasium, and sauna/whirlpool. Heritage Hall houses meeting rooms and the office of the activity director. Tennis courts are in the western sector. Over one hundred activities are available, covering everything from bocci to the yacht and model clubs. The developer retained ownership of the eighteen-hole and nine-hole golf courses, which charge fees that residents feel are reasonable.

Village administration is more complicated than in most other RCs of this size. All of the individual 2,580 units (4,200 residents) are grouped into twenty-four condominiums. Each condominium is a separate legal entity, has its own offices, and elects a trustee to represent its residents on the Heritage Village Master Association. Extensive brochures are issued to residents that explain how the village operates and what is involved in owning a unit in a condominium. The master association is responsible for the operation, maintenance, and repair of the common facilities, which includes the exterior of all residential buildings.

We had a long conversation with Bill Woodward, president of the master association and a resident for eight years. He explained to us that running the village is big business: the annual budget is nine million dollars, and there are 103 full-time employees, plus 50 part-time.

Two major changes took place recently to ensure the future stability of the community:

1. A professionally trained and experienced city manager has been hired, through a search agency, to serve as chief executive. He will report to the Board of the Master Association.
2. A special Long Range Planning Committee has been assigned the responsibility of developing a fifteen-year plan.

Heritage Village Real Estate Company supplied us with resale prices and estimated monthly costs. Following are three examples:

UNIT	PRICE	MONTHLY COSTS*
Carriage House—1 floor		
1 bedroom, 1 bath,	$ 65,000 (+)	
955 sq. ft.		$477.88
Sherman—1 floor		
2 bedrooms, 2 baths,		
1,427 sq. ft.	125,000 (+)	657.71
Villager—2 floors		
2 bedrooms, 2½ baths,		
1,550 sq. ft.	150,000 (+)	653.18

*Costs include *common charges* (maintenance of building exterior, community and neighborhood common areas; electricity including heat; sewer and water; and taxes).

Bill said that the community is going through a transition. The "early" owners are now in their seventies and eighties. Many original residents have moved to life-care communities, which has created an increase in the number of homes for sale. Logically, this trend will continue. Additionally, the newcomers in their early to mid-sixties have a different outlook on community living. It is normal that new views and ideas on how to run the community will be forthcoming. Adjustments will have to be made regardless of how difficult they may be.

Betty Ferry, a longtime friend of ours and a twenty-year resident, echoed the feelings of Bill Woodward. Her concern was the decline in the number of volunteers to

CLIMATE—1991 TEMP. (°F), PRECIP. (IN.)				OF INTEREST—
	AVG.	MAX.	MIN.	PRECIP.
JAN.	27.0	49	1	2.45
APR.	53.3	90	28	3.54
JULY	73.7	101	50	2.90
OCT.	55.1	79	28	3.17

OF INTEREST— Total precipitation in 1991 was 47.26 inches during the winter, rain often falls through cold air trapped in the Connecticut River Valley, creating hazardous ice conditions.

take the place of those leaving the community or "retiring" from such duties as driving the ambulance. She remains quite involved in village and town activities and feels very positive about the community.

The two aggressive actions taken by the board should ensure the stability of this mature village as it experiences a changing of the guard—very similar to what is happening in our government and in many corporations.

Heritage Village Master Association, Inc., The Meeting House, One Heritage Way, Southbury, CT 06488 203/264-7570

MOUNTAINBROOK VILLAGE, GOLD CANYON, ARIZONA

A Jewel in the Rough

In the foothills of the Superstition Mountains, and the east Phoenix Valley, is an adult community unlike any other we have surveyed. At an elevation of 1,800 feet, the

All homes at MountainBrook Village have concrete tile roofs and stucco exteriors.

temperature is five to ten degrees cooler than in the low desert. All that can be seen to the south, east, and west is undeveloped desert. Looking north toward the mountains is the Gold Canyon Resort and Conference Center, protected by saguaros with outstretched arms that seem to say "Beware."

Not far away is the Apache Trail, used by Apache Indians as a shortcut through the Superstition Mountains to reach early Salt River Valley settlements. Legend has it that these mountains also hide the Lost Dutchman Gold Mine.

But MountainBrook Village isn't really in the middle of nowhere. Apache Junction (pop. 18,130) is only eight miles to the west, downtown Mesa is twenty miles, and Sky Harbor International Airport in Phoenix is thirty-five miles away. Within two miles is a fire station with ambulance and paramedic service, and a hospital is fifteen miles away. Five miles to the west is a gas station and convenience store.

Unfortunately, this pristine ruggedness is likely to change in the coming years. The thirty-mile Superstition Freeway, a superhighway connecting to I-10 in Phoenix, was completed in 1993. Current residents expect this ease of travel to draw more homeowners to the area, which will affect the seclusion and small population that exist today.

The developer is UDC Homes, Inc., which is listed on the New York Stock Exchange and headquartered in Arizona. The total area of MountainBrook Village is 600 acres; 320 homes have been sold, with room for a total of 1,700 homes. Build-out is expected by 1999.

The nearby fifty-six-unit Gold Canyon Resort and Conference Center, with restaurant, semiprivate eighteen-hole, par-seventy-one, 6,398-yard golf course, two lighted tennis courts, and stables, is also owned by UDC Homes, Inc.

Residents choose from ten different floor plans and thirty exterior designs. All homes have a concrete tile roof, stucco exterior, and General Electric appliances in the kitchen.

Prices are as follows:

Saguaro: 1,426 sq. ft.—2 bedrooms/2 baths $90,990

Jasmine: 1,581 sq. ft.—2 or 3 bedrooms/2 baths $102,990

Acacia: 2,151 sq. ft.—2 or 3 bedrooms/2 baths $123,990

Ocotillo: 2,317 sq. ft.—2 or 3 bedrooms/2 baths $127,990

All homes have a two-car garage and prices include a standard lot. Homes built on the golf course or with panoramic views are more expensive. Yearly homeowners association dues are $385 per household.

The developers have taken great care to retain the natural terrain; only 15 percent of the community-owned land has been disturbed. Homes are placed to blend in with the varied topography. Roads into some areas have a steep incline.

The one-story village activity center, completed in mid-1992, has a large central meeting room, areas for arts and crafts, a billiards room, a library, and an exercise room. Adjacent is a heated thirty-by-sixty-foot pool and hot tub.

A MountainBrook Village at Gold Canyon residents association currently is in the organizing and develop-

---

CLIMATE—1991 TEMP. (°F), PRECIP. (IN.)

	AVG.	MAX.	MIN.	PRECIP.
JAN.	55.9	76	36	0.63
APR.	72.2	97	49	0.00
JULY	95.1	112	72	0.14
OCT.	80.2	105	46	1.16

OF INTEREST—

The temperature at MountainBrook Village generally is 5 to 10 degrees lower than in Phoenix. Thunderstorms peak in July and August.

ment stage. Architectural, activities, budget and finance, building and grounds, communications and newsletter, legislation, and welcome committees are in place. A monthly newsletter keeps residents informed of the activity schedule, which includes tennis, golf, educational programs, water exercise, ladies' bridge, ladies' aerobics, bingo, a men's coffee group every morning except Sunday, a weekly men's noon social and luncheon, and the community happy hour each Tuesday evening.

Residents receive a discount on greens fees at the Gold Canyon Resort and can use the tennis courts at no charge. Through a series of back trails, golf carts can be driven to the club without having to traverse the main roads. A golf course within the community is in the long-range plan.

When UDC owns 25 percent or less of the community land, it will begin turning over ownership of the community to the residents association.

Residents report that every afternoon, winds blow down out of the mountains. During our visit the wind brought along thunderheads, and by 5:00 P.M. the entire northern sky was one heavy black mass with high swirling winds kicking up dust in the flatlands. It looked ominous, but as we drove west along the Superstition Freeway, the threatening clouds seemed to be contained by the mountains. We encountered some high winds but no rain.

For those who do not want an RC that resembles city living, and are willing to put a few extra miles on the odometer, foothills living at MountainBrook Village might be ideal.

MountainBrook Village, 5674 S. Marble Dr., Gold Canyon, AZ 85219
800/950-4832

PINE LAKES COUNTRY CLUB, NORTH FORT MYERS, FLORIDA

Affordable Retirement Housing

Pine Lakes is the offspring of an adjacent RC called Lake Fairways. Both manufactured-housing communities have golf courses and are attractively designed.

For years Florida has touted its affordable retirement housing. This has translated into hundreds, perhaps thousands, of manufactured-housing developments. Virtually all are built on a grid design, tend to be crowded, and lack distinction, but they are affordable.

What drew us to Lake Fairways and then Pine Lakes was their unusual layout. Homes are built in cul-de-sacs around a golf course and a series of lakes. Most cul-de-sacs have twelve homes, which lends a neighborhood atmosphere to each housing cluster. The monthly publication, *Whispering Pines,* features stories about a variety of community clubs, including singles, tennis, bowling, ladies' and men's golf, and bridge.

Residents organize all activities, which in recent years have included an evening with the Ink Spots, a country-western hoedown country fair, and A Taste of Pine Lakes,

The clubhouse complex at Pine Lakes features a large auditorium, exercise and crafts rooms, a swimming pool, and tennis courts.
(PHOTO COURTESY OF PINE LAKES COUNTRY CLUB)

a sampling of gourmet specialties from a dozen local restaurants.

We met with four residents for an open, candid roundtable discussion about Pine Lakes. One couple said they chose Pine Lakes in part because they liked the climate, cleanliness, and lack of congestion on the southwest coast of Florida. Other factors were the cul-de-sac design, which they said fosters friendliness, and the average resident age of fifty-nine to sixty, which gives them all the opportunity to become good friends as they grow old together. All four of these residents had taken early retirement and were in their early sixties. All also held jobs in the community and did volunteer work as well.

When we asked about the management, these couples said that the developers were fair and listened when the residents association made a suggestion. For example, an awning recently had been installed over part of the pool patio at residents' request, prompted by the medical profession's warnings about overexposure to the sun's rays.

We next met with Bob Brown, a principal in the ownership of both communities, who told us that about 75 percent of the 866 Pine Lakes homesites have homes completed or under construction. When we asked what would happen when this community was completed, he replied, "We'll build another one."

Pine Lakes residents must buy and build their own home, but they can choose to buy or rent the land. According to Bob Brown, "You can pay a rent of $350 a month, or pay $35,000 for the land. Sixty-five percent of the residents have a lifetime lease on the land, and thirty-five percent of them purchase."

These two options require a complete analysis of what is and isn't included in each option. Leases start at $250 a month, and a 7,500-square-feet lot starts at $23,900. In both options there are many inclusions and exclusions regarding maintenance, taxes, and utility payments. Legal guidance is advisable.

Homes range from a base cost of $59,990 to $83,990. Golf membership (eighteen-hole par-sixty-one) costs $900 annually for one person, $1,380 for a family; the annual trail fee for private golf carts is an extra $525. We

CLIMATE—1991 TEMP. (°F), PRECIP. (IN.)				OF INTEREST—
	AVG.	MAX.	MIN.	PRECIP.
JAN.	70.3	87	46	7.95
APR.	77.7	95	58	5.01
JULY	83.0	96	71	14.51
OCT.	78.0	94	57	4.01

OF INTEREST— Two-thirds of the annual precipitation occurs from June through September. During this same period thunderstorms occur two out of every three days on average, but seldom a day goes by without sun.

asked Mr. Brown about the sturdiness of the manufactured homes. He said, "We have had some very rough weather here and haven't had any trouble."

Pine Lakes is located on Route 41 about eight miles north of Fort Myers. One shopping center is six miles south, and another is twelve miles north. Open space surrounds the two communities, which impressed us as informal, down-to-earth RCs. Indicative of this is the occasional "turn-the-table" party, when Bob Brown does the serving of the meal. Maintenance of the common grounds and individual lots is good.

The clubhouse has a large auditorium and rooms for exercise, billiards, cards, and crafts. The heated swimming pool, Jacuzzi, and tennis courts offer opportunities for a well-rounded retirement experience.

Pine Lakes Country Club, P.O. Box 3494, North Fort Myers, FL 33918
813/731-5555   800/237-8908

On the golf course at Radnor Sun Village, water comes into play on nine holes.   (PHOTO BY KEN EASLEY)

RADNOR SUN VILLAGE, SURPRISE, ARIZONA

A Surprise in the Desert

While we were surveying Edgewater Landing in Florida (see page 86), Marty Berge told us of another Radnor Corporation RC in Surprise, Arizona. Radnor is a wholly-owned subsidiary of The Sun Company, number fifty-nine in the Fortune 500 listing. Because we were impressed with Edgewater Landing, we included Sun Village on our list of Arizona RCs to survey.

In Phoenix we perused the housing section of the Sunday paper and saw a large ad for Sun Village announcing a bonus of a three hundred-square-foot detached guest house ($15,400 value) with the purchase of a single-family home. We let our imaginations run wild as we made up a list of uses for a freestanding small house with one bedroom, bath, and closet:

Multiuse with Murphy bed	Hobby room
for guests	Music studio
Mother or Dad's room	Game room
Grandchildren's playroom	Art studio
Library for the scholar/writer	Exercise
Office/computer room	TV center

Over the years we have advocated the importance of a private space for each person to do his or her own "thing," and a detached room offers an ideal solution if home space is limited.

Sun Village, an age-restricted community (fifty-five-plus), is situated northwest of Phoenix on 320 acres along Bell Road, about three miles beyond Sun City West. Shopping, medical services, and a hospital are all within five miles of Sun Village, and the new Arrowhead Regional Shopping Center is eleven miles to the east. Sky Harbor Airport is forty miles away in Phoenix, where Interstates 17 and 10 intersect.

Across from the community's guarded entrance is a large orange grove, and in the vicinity are many vegetable and fruit farms. Undeveloped desert provides a southwest vista, with the White Tanks Mountains in the background.

Winding through the community is an eighteen-hole golf course with many water hazards—water comes into play on nine holes.

There are three housing options in this affordable community:

CASITAS—2 models:

936 sq. ft., $64,500; 935 sq. ft., $65,500. Association fee $107.94 a month, includes landscaping, all exterior maintenance, required insurance on common areas, and water.

PATIO HOMES—4 models:

Midsize 1,236 sq. ft., $82,900. Association fee $104.92 a month, includes front yard landscaping and maintenance, exterior painting, use of Zuni Village Club House, and pool.

SINGLE FAMILY HOMES—7 models:

1,292 sq. ft. to 2,237 sq. ft., priced from $96,900 to $139,900. Includes standard lot. Association fee $39.73 a month.

Adjacent to the 47,000-square-foot recreation center is a large, heated outdoor pool. Inside the center are meeting rooms, a lounge, arts and crafts studios, library, a billiards room, restaurant, and hair salon. The community schedule is crowded with such activities as tennis and golf tournaments, seminars, parties, trips, and Friday afternoon happy hour.

CLIMATE—1991 TEMP. (°F), PRECIP. (IN.)				OF INTEREST—
	AVG.	MAX.	MIN.	PRECIP.
JAN.	55.9	76	36	0.63
APR.	72.2	97	49	0.00
JULY	95.1	112	72	0.14
OCT.	80.2	105	46	1.16

OF INTEREST— Elevation is 1,100 feet in the Sonoran Desert. Total precipitation in 1991 was 8.35 inches. Thunderstorms peak in July and August.

Lee Kammeyer, president of the residents association, told us that build-out would probably happen in late 1994. He said that the three different purchasing options make it difficult to project the future because of the uncertainty of buyer preference. Sales are good, and he was optimistic about the future. We felt that this somewhat compact community of affordable home options would be a good desert retirement haven.

Radnor Sun Village, 14300 W. Bell Rd., Surprise, AZ 85374
602/271-4242   800/654-9969

SUNBIRD GOLF RESORT, CHANDLER, ARIZONA

"I'll Stay Here"

Cliff and Karen Thomas moved to SunBird from South Carolina. They say people often ask why they left their home state, especially since they owned a house on a

The SunBird Golf Resort, designed for active adults, includes the SunBird recreation complex overlooking the pool and spa. (PHOTO BY STEVE CUTTER)

large lot that faced a river. They both emphatically answered, "Yard work, humidity, and mosquitoes!"

Two months after their move-in, Cliff, an avid tennis player, collapsed on the courts as a result of a blood clot. Other players administered CPR until the paramedics arrived, and his condition was touch-and-go on the twelve-minute ambulance ride to the hospital.

Fortunately, he recovered with very little damage to his heart. Thirty-five days later he was back playing tennis, and when we saw him he was the picture of health.

Karen emotionally described the response of the entire community during Cliff's illness. "We were still new arrivals, yet everyone made us feel that we had been close friends for years—we couldn't believe it!" She compared the community to an extended family, and said that even when Cliff's prognosis was uncertain, she told her neighbors, "I'll stay here."

Robson Communities bought this 320-acre facility, which had been a manufactured housing development, when the original developer went bankrupt. They then opened under the SunBird banner in 1990. Since that time, all housing is built on-site. There are 700 homes, and at build-out there will be 1,600. When completed, the complex will be owned by the residents association. One member of each household must be at least forty years old, and no one is permitted in permanent residence under age nineteen.

This gated community is located three miles south of the city of Chandler and twenty-six miles southeast of downtown Phoenix. I-10 is six miles to the west.

SunBird has two series of houses—four models of Casita homes and five models of Classic homes—each with choices of exterior elevations. Cost includes a standard lot. The Casita homes have a covered carport with a fully maintained Xeriscape greenbelt in back, complete with a paved golf cart path.

BALBOA (smallest):
908 sq. ft.—2 bedrooms/2 baths $62,700

TAHOE (largest):
972 sq. ft.—2 bedrooms/2 baths, golf cart, garage
$66,300

The Classic homes are made of stucco with cement tile roofs, the normal desert architecture, and attached two-car garage.

VENTURA: 1,011 sq. ft.—2 bedrooms/2 baths $78,500

CATALINA: 1,320 sq. ft.—2 bedrooms/2 baths $87,050

GRANADA: 1,680 sq. ft.—2 bedrooms/2 baths, study
$103,550

Homeowners association dues are $35 per month for each household.

The uniqueness of SunBird is a forty thousand-square-foot, three-level recreation complex overlooking the pool and eighteen-hole executive golf course. The complex is exceptionally large for the size of the community, with sloping, curving walkways to the large heated pool and spa. There are porches around the upper levels, and patio areas surround the pool. Not too far away is a smaller swimming pool.

Inside are rooms for arts and crafts, a library, billiards, exercise, sauna and lockers, card games, a post office, administrative offices, lounges, a bar and grill, and a grand ballroom that is larger than the ballrooms at many major hotels. One large area of the building has not been renovated—a treasure trove for future activities. There is also a driving range and lighted tennis courts.

Karen told us that there is plenty of shopping within a few miles, and that in addition to activities at SunBird residents can participate in activities that take place in Chandler, a town of over 90,000 people. We reviewed two

CLIMATE—1991 TEMP. (°F), PRECIP. (IN.)				OF INTEREST—
	AVG.	MAX.	MIN.	PRECIP.	Elevation is 1,100 feet in the Sonora Desert.
JAN.	55.9	76	36	0.63	Total precipitation in
APR.	72.2	97	49	0.00	1991 was 8.35 inches.
JULY	95.1	112	72	0.14	Thunderstorms peak in
OCT.	80.2	105	46	1.16	July and August.

issues of the monthly community paper, *SunBird Views*, which included a daily schedule of activities such as water aerobics, body toning, Tappercise, square/line/round dancing, SunBird Singers, Bible class, seminars, computer courses, art workshop, rug classes, block party egg hunt, pizza party, monthly potluck dinner, plus many sporting events.

Cliff said he feels the homeowners council is effective. There are seven committees and the minutes of the monthly council meeting are published. When asked what he would change if he could, he replied, "I wish that more people stayed here during the summer." In regions as warm as this one gets, perhaps the retirement saying "run to the sun" should be change to "run to and from the sun."

We had the feeling that this relatively inexpensive community was still growing and organizing. The future looks bright.

SunBird Golf Resort, 6250 SunBird Blvd., Chandler, AZ 85249
602/732-1000   800/523-6664

SUN CITY TUCSON, TUCSON, ARIZONA

The Smallest Sun City

We asked Jack and Sherry Redosky, five-year residents of Sun City Tucson (SCT), why they moved to Arizona from California. "Because of the high cost of living," they said, "there is no way we could retire in California." They looked at many parts of Arizona, and chose the Tucson area because of the higher altitude (3,000 feet) and cooler temperatures, the nearness of the Santa Catalina Mountains, and the rural setting of SCT.

When we visited, residents mentioned that "monsoon season" was coming soon. We checked the *Arizona Almanac,* and sure enough, monsoons (the local term for brief, heavy rainstorms) are most pronounced in southern Arizona. The wettest and longest season in recent years was 1984, with ninety-nine monsoon days. The average is fifty-seven days.

SCT, a 1,000-acre development, is located ten miles northwest of Tucson in Pima County. The eighteen-hole golf course fills 130 acres, and 300 acres will remain open space. There are currently 2,320 residents with about 5,000 expected at build-out in three to four years. One resident in each household must be at least fifty-five, and no one is permitted in permanent residence under nineteen years of age. Visits from children are limited to ninety days a year. The average resident age is sixty-three.

Arizona desert views are a daily indulgence at Sun City Tucson.
(PHOTO COURTESY OF DEL WEBB'S SUN CITIES)

The community has a fire station with ambulance and paramedic services on-site. Northwest Hospital in Tucson is twelve miles away. Emergency service is available in Catalina, five miles away. A 275-member "volunteer posse" patrols the community nightly, and the Oro Valley Police Department has never received a report of a crime at SCT.

Adjacent to the entrance is Mountain View Plaza, covering 28,000 square feet. Tenants include a hair salon, home health center, physician and dentist offices, restaurant/bakery, Minit Market, golf cart shop, and specialty shops.

SCT has two resident-owned and -operated recreation centers valued at $6.5 million. The main center, Mountain Vista, is located on a knoll overlooking the golf course, and has a spectacular panoramic view of the mountains. The Desert Oasis Center is located among the neighborhoods. Amenities within these two centers include:

475-seat multipurpose auditorium	Double Eagle Grille
6 multipurpose meeting rooms	3 warming kitchens
Kachina Lounge	Table tennis
Billiards room	Racquetball courts
2 outdoor heated pools	Basketball courts
Indoor therapy pool	Library
8 tennis courts, 6 lighted	Computer center
2 lighted shuffleboard courts	Village store
7 lighted bocci ball courts	Lapidary (gem cutting)
9-hole miniature golf course	Arts (painting)
Pro shop	Woodcarving
Fully equipped exercise room	Stained glass
	Ceramics
	Silversmithing
	Sewing
	Woodworking shop

Jogging track/par exercise course Locker room facilities Horseshoe pits	Pottery studio Etching, wood block, and lino cuts

Included among the chartered clubs and organizations are art, bocci, book, Bible study, bridge (partners, ladies, duplicate, couples), ceramics, computer, Spanish language, energetic exercise, garden, genealogy, golf, pottery, photography, patrol and neighborhood watch, singers, racquetball, table tennis, and tap dance.

There are sixteen model homes in three categories of size and price:

DESERT COLLECTION—5,000 sq. ft. homesites, 4 models
Oasis (smallest): 1,093 sq. ft.—2 bedrooms, 1½ bath, den, 1½-car garage $87,900

CANYON COLLECTION—6,000 sq. ft. homesites, 6 models
Madera (midsize): 1,779 sq. ft.—2 bedrooms, 2 baths, Arizona room, 2-car garage $138,300

CATALINA COLLECTION—7,000 sq. ft. homesites, 6 models
Tortolita (largest): 2,630 sq. ft.—2 master suites, 2 baths, powder room, Arizona room, den, 2-car garage, golf cart garage $189,900

Homeowners association dues are $320 a year.

SCT opened in January 1987 and was rejuvenated in July 1989 when a new general manager was appointed. His first task was to fire forty employees, as a result of resident discontent. He then held a residents meeting with only one staff person present to take notes. There was one ground rule: "Nobody raises his or her voice." More than one hundred resident comments, written and oral, were responded to within three weeks. Communications were opened and appear to remain that way.

The May 1993 residents' newsletter reported the organizing of two committees, architectural review and deed restriction enforcement. The newsletter also included activity announcements for forty clubs and organizations, and two seminars entitled, "Living with Wildlife: Coping with Critters" and "Landscaping for Wildlife." Residents are learning to resolve gardening conflicts with urban javelinas, coyotes, woodpeckers, and other desert animals.

SCT is surrounded by miles of open spaces in all directions. Those wanting a sense of freedom and exceptional vistas would find this an ideal community to visit. As we toured the community and talked with many res-

CLIMATE—1991 TEMP. (°F), PRECIP. (IN.)				OF INTEREST—
	AVG.	MAX.	MIN.	PRECIP.	Temperatures above
JAN.	52.3	74	26	1.15	90°F prevail from May through September,
APR.	65.2	92	37	0.00	with an average of 41
JULY	87.5	109	67	0.44	days at 100°F or higher.
OCT.	74.0	100	36	0.73	Half of the annual precipitation (10.78 inches in 1991) falls between July 1 and September 15.

idents, it appeared that morale is good and the people are happy. Just don't try to pet the coyotes!

Sun City Tucson, 13990 N. Desert Butte Rd., Tucson, AZ 85737

602/825-5900   800/422-8483

RETIREMENT COMMUNITIES—
1,000 OR FEWER RESIDENTS

In order to build the big RCs, developers first must find large tracts of land.

A parcel of land suitable for building one hundred or more houses, however, or a congregate living complex with cottages, can be found much closer to town. Small communities give residents easy accessibility to city conveniences and services.

Small retirement communities have their share of amenities and activities, but these generally are not as broad in scope as in the larger communities. However, residents report a strong feeling of belonging in a small community of people with like needs. Communities in this chapter include age-restricted (fifty-five-plus) housing as well as congregate living communities with home care and/or assisted living. Communities with intermediate and skilled nursing are listed in Chapter 7.

CARRIAGE CLUB, CHARLOTTE, NORTH CAROLINA

Innovation Plus

When we arrived at Carriage Club, we found Activity Director Betsy Seymour perched on top of a ten-foot ladder directly beneath a beautiful chandelier. "We're decorating for our fifth anniversary party next Sunday," she said. "Be great if you could join us—we'll have a great party."

Carriage Club is a forty-five-acre rental retirement commuity in a wooded area on the outskirts of Charlotte, North Carolina.

Her enthusiasm, positive outlook, and endless energy were clear as she raced down the steps to greet us. In no time we felt like old friends. As we talked we were interrupted frequently by passersby who greeted Betsy and chatted about her project.

Betsy told us some of her innovative ideas for entertaining residents. For example:

1. Because there are three women for every man at Carriage Club (CC), she follows the pattern of cruise ships and hires men of the appropriate age to attend the popular monthly dances.
2. She rented a cow and a pig to accent theme parties.
3. Residents receive a colorful balloon at their mailbox on their birthday. We saw one lady in the pool wearing a pink balloon tied to her wrist.
4. Two to three entertainment evenings a week bring professional performers to display their talents.

A community shuttle bus makes frequent runs around the grounds, and residents who prefer to walk enjoy the long enclosed, carpeted, heated/air-conditioned bridge across the lakes. The bridge has huge windows and fishing porches so residents can observe fish, frogs, and turtles in the water. One resident told us she uses the bridge as her exercise course when it's too hot or too cold outside.

Eckerd Drugs has a store on-site with a snack bar and mini-mart that serves as a pick-up point for prescription drugs.

CC is a forty-five-acre rental RC with a minimum age

of sixty-two. Assisted living is available in thirty units. There are five apartment buildings on one side of the two lakes; on the other side are two apartment buildings and the villas. Three hundred residents reside in the 176 individual units. There is no entrance fee. Monthly rental and service fees are as follows:

Studio apartment (527 sq. ft.):	$1,140–1,290
1 bedroom, 1½ bath (807 sq. ft.):	$1,575–1,650
2 bedrooms, 2 baths, deluxe (1,140 sq. ft.):	$1,790–2,040
Villa, 2 bedrooms, 2 baths (1,372 sq. ft.):	$2,160–2,245
Second person charge	$375

These fees include emergency call service and nursing service, weekly housekeeping, apartment and grounds maintenance, local scheduled transportation, gated security, garden plots, and twenty-five meals per month (lunch or dinner), all utilities except telephone.

Assisted living in the Coach House is available, with a private apartment and bathroom for $2,150 per month (second person, $500) and offering emergency nursing and aides around the clock, three meals a day in the Coach House dining room, housekeeping weekly or as needed, assistance in normal daily activities such as bathing and dressing, monitoring of drugs, and scheduled transportation to doctors and planned activities.

Community amenities at CC include a lounge; auditorium; exercise room; heated pool and Jacuzzi; TV room; library; chapel; card room; private dining room; arts and crafts studio; croquet, shuffleboard, and horseshoe courts;

billiards room; bank; beauty/barber shop; lighted walking trails; and many conversation areas.

CC is run by American Retirement Corporation, a major company in retirement community management. The company conducts quarterly resident opinion polls and distributes the findings to all concerned.

This community is located in Charlotte, which is in the southwestern part of North Carolina, very near the South Carolina border. Population in 1990 was 395,934, and it is the largest city in the state.

CC is in a heavily wooded area in the southern outskirts of the city. Charlotte-Douglas International Airport is west of Charlotte and is easily reached via the loop around the city. Downtown is approximately five miles away, and local shopping is within two miles. North-south I-77 and east-west I-85 intersect in Charlotte.

While touring the facility we chatted with five ladies enjoying the pool, and they couldn't say enough about the community: "The staff breaks their neck for you," "There is something for everyone," "If a person can't be happy here, they can't be happy anyplace," and "Good bunch of people—very friendly." All five of them agreed that having a washer and dryer in each apartment was "the best."

Betsy arranged a lunch for us with five other residents, three women and two men, all of whom said that the friendliness of the people was the best thing about Carriage Club. Dick Eldredge, a member of the residents association board and former president of the twenty-member Ambassador Club, said that getting new residents off to a good start is the key to resident friendliness. He sent us a copy of the Ambassador Club New Resident Orientation Worksheet. Two club members are assigned to each new resident or couple, and all members are informed of the newcomers' arrival date, apartment, and phone number. The welcoming process starts with a lunch or dinner to meet the other residents; thirty informational items are covered and special attention is paid to the newcomers for the first month. New residents have their pictures taken and posted on the bulletin board. Tuesday morning coffee hour and the social hour before dinner also help residents get acquainted. Dick said there is a great deal of commitment among the members of the Ambassador Club.

No major issues have caused any conflict between management and the residents. A recent dispute over how the vegetables were cooked resulted in a new option on the form residents fill out for each meal. In the vegetable category, it offers a choice between "northern crisp" style and "southern well done."

CLIMATE—1991 TEMP. (°F), PRECIP. (IN.)				OF INTEREST—
	AVG.	MAX.	MIN.	PRECIP.
JAN.	43.1	65	22	6.02
APR.	64.4	86	40	5.43
JULY	82.2	99	67	3.70
OCT.	63.5	85	40	0.50

OF INTEREST—
Elevation is 730 feet.
Temperatures can be as low as 32°F on half of the days in the winter months, but snow is infrequent. Total precipitation in 1991 was 45.18 inches.

We made more new friends at lunch, and when we thanked Betsy we received a farewell hug.

Carriage Club of Charlotte, 5700 Old Providence Rd., Charlotte, NC 28226
704/366-4960

CHAMBREL AT CLUB HILL, GARLAND, TEXAS

At Your Service

We table-hopped during continental breakfast at Chambrel and talked with ten to fifteen residents. Conversations went like this:

Gentleman: "This is the fourth community I've lived at in the Dallas area and this is by far the best." Why? "It's the staff—they go way beyond the call of duty." Another group of five all echoed his comments—"Everybody is somebody."

Lady: "I still own my home [in a suburb] but my son doesn't want me to live there alone in a two-story house. I've lived here over a year and I like it, but I'm looking for a man to live with me in my home—so far no luck!"

Gentleman from Assisted Living: "At the place I lived before, during meals, some of the people took a nap between each bite. It's different here—it's lively, and the 'at your service' motto really works. I've panned gold in Alaska, ridden a camel in the desert, gone swimming in

Residents of Chambrel at Club Hill enjoy each other's company in one of the model cottages. (PHOTO BY JEFF LAYDON)

the Sea of Galilee, and I'm one of those people who are going to live to a hundred."

Gentleman: "I have family nearby, but sometimes they get in the way. This is my family here."

We first visited Chambrel in September 1987 at the time of its grand opening. Six years later the buildings and grounds looked as fresh and neat as they did on our first visit.

Situated northeast of Dallas in the suburb of Garland,

Chambrel is a full-service rental community on eleven acres, two miles from the Garland central business district and ten miles from downtown Dallas. The community borders the upscale Club Hill residential area and is one mile from the Eastern Hills Country Club. Shopping is five minutes away. The Oxford Services Company, part of the Oxford Development Corporation founded in 1949, owns and operates eight Chambrel communities throughout the country.

The community has a total of 259 homes: 216 garden apartments, 16 cottages, and 27 assisted living apartments. It is 95 percent occupied, and the average age is seventy-eight. The minimum age requirement is fifty-five.

MONTHLY RENTAL—APARTMENT

1 bedroom/1 bath, 481 sq. ft., $1,250
1 bedroom/1 bath/den, 726 sq. ft., $1,550
1 bedroom/1 bath deluxe, 663 sq. ft., $1,450
2 bedrooms/2 baths, 895 sq. ft., $1,750

Includes utilities (except telephone), one meal plus continental breakfast, weekly flat linen service, housekeeping every two weeks, basic cable TV, medical alert system.

COTTAGE

2 bedrooms/2 baths, 998 sq. ft., $2,120
2 bedrooms/2 baths, 1,150 sq. ft., $2,350

For a second person, apartment and cottage, add $325. Includes same services as apartments except for continental breakfast, and housekeeping every other week. Without meals, flat linen services, and housekeeping, cottages cost $1,850 and $2,175 (one or two persons).

Amenities include use of the dining room, library, pool/spa, music room, greenhouse, lounge, billiard room, art studio, meeting rooms, beauty/barber salon, transportation and activity programs run by a professional activity director.

The September calendar we saw included announcements for many exercise classes, a line dance, oil painting, china painting, card games, bingo, a Labor Day picnic, dinner out, movies, a community meeting, shopping trips, seminars, personal fitness instruction, entertainment, a birthday party, sewing circle, book club, new residents' reception, walking club, Hawaiian-style social hour, on-site Sunday afternoon worship service, and the Chambrel Searchers study club.

The grounds feature a pond, large fountain, and gazebo on gently rolling terrain. Covered walkways that connect the four multistory apartment buildings and the assisted-living complex to the clubhouse give shelter in difficult weather.

CLIMATE—1991 TEMP. (°F), PRECIP. (IN.)				OF INTEREST—
	AVG.	MAX.	MIN.	PRECIP.	Winters are mild;
JAN.	42.8	72	23	2.72	northers (storms) occur about three times each
APR.	67.4	93	42	3.63	month with sudden
JULY	85.0	101	67	3.99	drops in temperature.
OCT.	68.1	97	34	9.32	

During breakfast a lady asked one of the men what he wanted from the buffet, then brought him breakfast and sat next to him. One of the men at the table told us, "She is being courted." Sixty years ago she probably would have blushed, but she just smiled as her partner said, "Who is being courted?" Everyone chuckled and they went on with their meal. It was good to see that even as the years accumulate, romantic relationships continue on.

Chambrel at Club Hill, 1245 Colonel Dr., Garland, TX 75043
214/278-8533

EDGEWATER LANDING, EDGEWATER, FLORIDA

Preserving Native Vegetation

About a third of the way down the east coast of Florida, beginning at Ponce de Leon Inlet and continuing south for 155 miles to Jupiter Inlet, is the Indian River Lagoon. Known as an "underwater rain forest," it is home to 300 species of birds, 680 species of fish, 1,300 species of vegetation, 2,700 animals, and 90,000 fishermen.

One mile of the Edgewater Landing community fronts on this treasure trove of nature. From the recreation center a long wooden pier juts into the lagoon, equipped with lights and running water to assist in cleaning the catch.

Part of the Edgewater Landing community borders the Indian River Lagoon on the east coast of Florida. (PHOTO BY JAMEY LANTZ)

Crab pots are tied to the pier, and nets are used when the shrimp are running. Further down the property is a private boat-launching ramp with adjacent reserved spaces for boats.

The plot plan of this three-year-old manufactured-housing community includes cul-de-sacs, winding roads, nature preserve areas, three lakes, and a mile and a half of natural shell walkway along the banks of the lagoon. While planning a house, developers make every effort to preserve native vegetation. If a big tree or patch of vegetation is in the way, it can be saved by adjusting the location of the house, garage, or patio. No two homesites are alike. Close to half of the trees on the original site have been preserved—no comparison to the many communities that have a few palm trees planted on bulldozed land.

Marty Berge is the on-site developer in partnership with Radnor Corporation, a wholly-owned subsidiary of the Sun Company, an integrated supplier of oil, gas, and other energy resources. Our meeting with Marty, a separate meeting with his sales manager, and a tour with Marty's wife, Priscilla, gave us a good insight into the makeup of this community. All residents own their houses and also own a share of all the common areas, including the recreation center, through the homeowners association. In two to four years, when the community is completed, the developer will move on and it will be completely self-governed.

"We have to continuously involve people in the operation of the community so they are fully prepared for the responsibility that goes with community ownership," Marty said. "I had my accountant go over financial details so they know what's ahead."

When we visited in 1993, 146 lots were available; 308 others had been sold and 265 homes built. Residents' feelings toward the community are evident in these statistics: in 1992, 23 percent of sales came from referrals, and in 1993 referrals accounted for 28 percent of sales. Costs of available lots range from $10,900 to $66,900, and residents can choose from 120 different floor plans. The average cost of a home is $60,000, but prices range from $45,000 to $75,000. Residents pay their own utilities, taxes, home insurance, and a monthly $54.45 homeowners association fee.

Pat Palmier, chairman of the homeowners association, and his wife, Lois, have been residents for three years. When Pat retired after thirty-six years in the air force, the couple spent a short time in Tucson, Arizona, then tried RVing, and finally chose the east coast of Florida to be near their two daughters.

They describe Edgewater Landing as a "great place" with interesting people, where "something is always going on." To be chairman of the homeowners association, Pat said, "you have to be a good listener." He says he receives few genuine complaints; gripes tend to come primarily from people having trouble adjusting to retirement.

Other than normal new-home construction problems that are easily resolved, Pat is satisfied with Palm Harbor manufactured housing. "Our main problem now is getting everything organized," he said, "so that when we take over the community at build-out, probably in two years, the transition will be smooth and efficient. There are a lot of qualified residents who are on our transition committee, so it should work out okay."

All activities are organized and run by residents. There are twenty-four clubs with numerous social functions such as Italian night potluck dinner with barbershop harmony entertainment, pancake breakfasts, and a Kentucky Derby celebration and dance. A monthly activity calendar and announcements on closed-circuit Channel 8 keep everyone informed.

The National Home Builders Association selected the Edgewater Landing Recreation Center as the finest one built in an RC in the United States in 1989. It has a large auditorium, club room with billiards, cards, bar, arts and crafts center, woodworking shop, and exercise room with Universal gym. There is a heated pool, tennis courts, a shuffleboard court, screened-in Jacuzzi, horseshoe courts with clay pits, a large patio, and a laundry room near the pool so residents can swim while doing their laundry.

Edgewater Landing is located off U.S. Route 1, one mile south of SR 442. Adequate shopping is on U.S. 1, and a hospital is three miles away. The community is twenty-five minutes from Daytona Beach, which has a regional airport, and three golf courses are within a fifteen-minute drive. Nearby New Smyrna Beach, a quaint old town with many of its original Victorian homes restored, has an excellent beach.

According to Marty Berge, "This is not a 'cookie cutter' community." He's right—it's a well-maintained, well-

CLIMATE—1991 TEMP. (°F), PRECIP. (IN.)				OF INTEREST—
	AVG.	MAX.	MIN.	PRECIP.
JAN.	63.4	87	34	2.25
APR.	73.7	92	47	5.57
JULY	82.5	95	72	11.97
OCT.	73.8	90	50	2.94

OF INTEREST—
Elevations range from 3 to 15 feet above mean sea level. The rainy season, from June to mid-October, produces about 60 percent of the annual rainfall, which was 67.19 inches in 1991.

designed community that emphasizes personal attention. Edgewater Landing is a good place to land.

Edgewater Landing, P.O. Box 1179, Edgewater, FL 32132
904/423-0221   800/635-2272

LA VIDA DEL MAR, SOLANA BEACH, CALIFORNIA

Innovative Health Care

One quarter of a mile from the Pacific Ocean, many of the one- and two-bedroom apartments at La Vida Del Mar have an ocean view. Looking to the east, at the end of Del Mar Downs Road, is Belmont Downs Horse Racing Track at the county fairgrounds. The tranquility of the ocean and the excitement of watching the ponies run are both available at this rental retirement community situated between the villages of Del Mar and Rancho Santa Fe, about twenty miles north of San Diego.

La Vida Del Mar is a small community of 105 apartments in a complex that looks more like a resort than a retirement community. The Mediterranean architecture is expansive, light, and airy, with custom-designed amenities such as conversation nooks and designer furnishings. The Grand Galleria is three stories high, with beautiful tapestries hanging from the beamed ceiling; it houses monthly art exhibitions as well. The Calypso dining room is partially circular in design, centering on columns set in a semicircle. A library and salon with fireplace are off of the Grand Galleria, as is an outdoor veranda.

There are three apartment styles available on a yearly lease basis:

PLAN I: 600 sq. ft.—1 bedroom, bath $1,845/month

PLAN II: 800 sq. ft.—1 bedroom, den, 2 baths
$2,225/month

PLAN III: 1,050 sq. ft.—2 bedrooms, 2 baths
$2,700/month

Additional resident $375/month

The Restaurant Terrace at La Vida Del Mar gives diners a view of the grounds.

Amenities included in the monthly fee are a restaurant, open twelve hours a day; lunch or dinner and breakfast; all utilities, including basic telephone and cable TV; weekly housekeeping; flat linen laundry service; twenty-four hour security service; free laundry facilities on each floor; a pool and spa; a full-time activities director; twenty-four-hour Lifeline emergency response service; and scheduled transportation. Pets are welcome.

The monthly activity schedule includes many movies, water exercise, exercise classes, weekly in-house banking, bridge lessons, trips to local attractions and activities, sing-a-longs, shopping, transportation to the doctor, chef chat, bingo, poetry readings, and happy hour every Friday afternoon.

Millie Bush, a resident, spoke with great enthusiasm about the community. She is active in a senior citizens group that meets at a nearby Presbyterian Church every Tuesday; their schedule is full enough to require four activity directors. She summed up her endorsement of the amenities and services this way: "It's handy as a pocket in your shirt."

Most of the residents are between seventy-five and eighty-five years of age. The residents association is not active, but there are monthly meetings of all residents, and management encourages the residents to reactivate the association. It's evident that the residents are very satisfied and don't feel the need for organized representation.

To keep residents living independently in apartments

and with friends as long as possible, the RC administration initiated an assistance program called AM/PM Support Care with Scripps Memorial Hospitals. Residents have a "menu" of support care to choose from based on their needs, and the counseling of an on-site registered nurse/case manager.

Services include assistance with walking, grooming, and personal services such as laundry and errands. Costs range from $15 an hour to $4 per fifteen-minute increment. The services are available twenty-four hours a day, seven days a week.

A semiprivate TLC (Temporary Living Care) Suite provides short-term respite nursing and/or convalescent care to those recovering from an injury or illness. A certified Scripps Howard nursing assistant is on duty twenty-four hours a day. Three meals are served at TLC for a daily cost of $125 per person.

As residents age, a retirement community needs to evaluate the services it provides. In some communities people must leave when they can no longer manage without assistance, and thus give up their friends and activi-

CLIMATE—1991 TEMP. (°F), PRECIP. (IN.)				OF INTEREST—
	AVG.	MAX.	MIN.	PRECIP.	85 percent of the annual rainfall occurs
JAN.	57.4	79	42	1.06	from November to
APR.	61.7	80	51	0.05	March. The highest
JULY	67.4	76	60	0.24	temperatures occur in
OCT.	68.0	92	48	0.69	September and October. Snow is rare.

ties. The management of La Vida Del Mar instead has seen fit to adjust their services to the changing needs of residents, thus keeping the support system intact as long as possible—in our opinion, the better way to go!

La Vida Del Mar, 850 Del Mar Downs Rd., Solana Beach, CA 92075
619/755-1224   800/445-2351 (inside California)

PLEASANT HILLS RETIREMENT COMMUNITY, LITTLE ROCK, ARKANSAS

Caring People Close at Hand

As we turned left on Napa Valley Road we knew we were in the high-rent district, a fine location for a retirement community. We drove through a gated entrance and around a three-story apartment building to the main building overlooking a forested valley. Connected cottages made of gray clapboard and stone surrounded the central building.

Our trip to Pleasant Hills was inspired by the title of their brochure, *Caring People Close at Hand.* It caught our attention, so we decided to survey and find out if it was true.

Lou Winchell, the executive director, greeted us and began to tell us about the community. While talking with us, she acknowledged a person near the door by smiling

Pleasant Hills cottages, apartments, and recreational buildings, such as this one, are made of stone and cedar.

and blowing a kiss. When she noticed our quizzical looks, she explained, "That was one of our residents who makes her rounds every morning to say hello. She's deaf." In order to communicate with this resident, staff members learned the fundamentals of sign language. The husband of a staff member located a nearby church that has a sign interpreter, and the resident is now an active participant there. Every Sunday morning a church member picks her up and takes her to services.

We were impressed with the care and devotion shown by the staff. Lou mentioned that she makes frequent visits to every resident who is hospitalized. Recently she visited a resident who had just been diagnosed with terminal cancer, and who asked, "Lou, can I go home to die?" The answer was "Of course, but with rules. If a time comes when we can't provide the necessary help, you will have to move to a nursing home." When we visited, this resident was comfortably settled upstairs in the personal care living area. There was no need to ask for terminally ill hospice assistance. The residents have responded with love and care for their seriously ill member of the community.

Pleasant Hills is a private rental community of 190 residents in 165 cottages and apartment-style homes. It uses ten acres of a twenty-acre plot. The first resident arrived in 1984 and is still in residence. The average age is eighty-two, and the oldest resident is ninety-nine.

HOME TYPE	SINGLE	TWO PEOPLE
Studio, 433 sq. ft.	$ 995	N/A
2 bedrooms/2 baths		
862 sq. ft.	1,420	1,645
Cottage, 2 bedrooms		
1,159 sq. ft.	1,390	1,475

Services provided include light breakfast and dinner (does not apply to cottage residents); emergency call system; housekeeping service every two weeks; all utilities except telephone and TV charges; scheduled transportation; use of the music room, library, and arts and crafts room; and free laundry facilities.

Residential care, which provides assistance with med-

CLIMATE—1991 TEMP. (°F), PRECIP. (IN.)				OF INTEREST—
	AVG.	MAX.	MIN.	PRECIP.	Winters are mild,
JAN.	39.0	59	18	6.88	although polar/arctic outbreaks are not
APR.	64.4	82	44	12.44	uncommon. Little or no
JULY	82.8	101	66	2.03	annual snowfall; ice
OCT.	64.3	86	41	7.00	storms infrequent.

ication, bathing, and dressing as needed, is more expensive.

A residents council meets monthly and a food committee discusses resident suggestions with management. Virtually all recommendations are implemented by management. The activity program is full but reflects the age of the residents, many of whom get around in three-wheel electric carts.

Extensive redecorating plans are scheduled for 1994. The facility is highly functional and serviceable, but is not plush. A plan is being developed to build a separate medical facility with assisted living. Fortunately there is a ten-acre plot available for this expansion.

Many of the staff have worked at Pleasant Hills for more than six years, and according to Lou the staff genuinely cares. This would be expected as a result of the leadership of Lou Winchell, a seventeen-year veteran administrator of care for the elderly.

Pleasant Hills Retirement Community, 800 Napa Valley Rd., Little Rock, AR 72211
501/225-9405

THE ISLAND ON LAKE TRAVIS, LAGO VISTA, TEXAS

Resort Retirement Living

As we drove up a hill and over a crest, a large body of blue water came into view. Completely covering a large island was a Mediterranean-style white stucco building with a large copper dome. This could have been an image from any country bordering the Mediterranean.

Instead, this was Hill Country, thirty-five miles west of Austin, Texas. We traveled on two-lane roads, up and

The Island on Lake Travis has 212 rental villas, each with a balcony.
(PHOTO COURTESY OF THE ISLAND ON LAKE TRAVIS)

down winding hills, through open cattle rangeland, and stopped once to avoid hitting three panicked deer. Finally we reached our destination, The Island.

We went down the hill to the visitor parking lot outside of the twenty-four-hour guarded gate, and then up the stairs to the second-floor marketing offices that are built over the causeway to the fourteen-acre Island.

Brenda Sullivan, marketing director, welcomed us and we started our survey of this unique retirement community. There are 212 rental villas, each with a balcony. The first residents arrived in late 1988, and it is now 90 percent occupied. The oldest resident is 93 and the average age is 68.7 years; 47 percent of the population are couples. There are no on-site health facilities. The Island is owned by the Chicago-based Prime Group, developers and investors in shopping malls, office buildings, parks, and retirement communities.

The causeway is one-eighth of a mile long and twelve feet above water level. To one side of the causeway is a marina with slips available to residents for $20 a month. Automobiles enter through one of three openings to a ground-level garage with spaces for four hundred cars. Because Hill Country flooding is possible, the first floor is three feet above the dam spillover level. During one severe flood the RC was evacuated for three days, and the floodwaters rose to the top of the garage. Fortunately, damage was minimal.

A glass-walled elevator took us to the first floor and our first conversation with a resident. As we looked over the four-foot-deep indoor lap pool a swimmer enthusiastically hollered, "It's a great place to live—I've been here four years." Her name was Jean Curry, and she moved to The Island from Rhode Island.

There are three floors of villas. Those facing the lake enjoy a clear view of the boat traffic. Across the water is a state park, which ensures that the natural beauty will be preserved. Villas facing the marina side overlook the water and a hill that is dotted with homes, whose lights make an attractive sight after dark.

Each villa opens onto a covered walkway that circles one of three beautifully landscaped patios featuring statuary, a pool or fountain, and well-placed spotlights. Fifty percent of the villas have wood-burning fireplaces, and wood is supplied at no charge.

A circular staircase provides an elegant entry to the dining room where we had an enjoyable lunch of soup and salad overlooking the lake. After lunch we met with nine residents, including the president of the residents council. Discussion included many comments about how secure residents feel. One person said that a neighbor checks on her if she is not up and about by 10:00 A.M. Others remarked on the beauty of the place, the two golf courses only a cart ride away, and a resident discount at one of them. Another person praised the family feeling: "They [the management] do everything to please you; I'm diabetic, and there are three sugar-free desserts."

We talked with the director of the "Fit for Life" program, an energetic, qualified young woman who helps individuals develop a fitness plan designed to meet their individual needs. She said she is amazed at the high degree of participation in the program.

Among the few complaints residents had, the two of most concern were the restrictive smoking policy (common areas are smoke-free) and the decision of the residents council to sell a fifty-one-foot yacht instead of making expensive needed repairs. Although these matters did not make everyone happy, most residents we spoke to felt the problems were inconsequential when compared to all the advantages of life on The Island.

Amenities and services at The Island include a full-service restaurant, private dining room, grand ballroom, lounge, library, arts and crafts room, indoor/outdoor pools, whirlpool and sauna, fitness center, billiards room, woodworking shop, convenience store, beauty and barber shops, banking services, lighted tennis courts, guest villas, weekly housekeeping, cable TV, all utilities (except telephone), transportation, indoor parking, an emergency response system, and cultural and social activities.

MONTHLY FEES—9 UNIT TYPES AVAILABLE

UNIT TYPE	MARINA VIEW	LAKE VIEW
Sheffield (1 bedroom)	N/A	$1,100
Portsmouth (1 bedroom)	$1,315	1,430
Manchester (1 bedroom/loft)	1,095	1,195
Barcelona (2 bedrooms)	1,675	1,745
Cayman (3 bedrooms)	N/A	2,625

Fees include all services and amenities plus continental breakfast daily and 240 meals per year (lunch or dinner); second person, $350 per month additional. Third-floor units with a panoramic view cost $50 additional per month.

The March 1993 activity calendar announced forty events away from The Island, including trips to five restaurants, league bowling, Weight Watchers, bingo, horse racing, a grocery and shopping mall trip each week, ballet and symphony performances in Austin, and special events.

On The Island, activities include bridge, canasta, bingo, "poverty poker," water volleyball, tap dance lessons, pool tournaments, fashion shows, low-impact aerobics, birthday parties, choir, residents council, art class, country-and-western dance lessons, and much more.

This is country living. Shopping, churches, and restaurants are not just around the corner. There is one doctor and an ambulance with paramedics in Lago Vista, and an

CLIMATE—1991 TEMP. (°F), PRECIP. (IN.)				OF INTEREST—
	AVG.	MAX.	MIN.	PRECIP.
JAN.	47.3	76	31	9.21
APR.	71.4	88	41	4.91
JULY	83.9	102	70	1.16
OCT.	72.7	98	40	3.06

OF INTEREST— Winters are mild; temperatures go below freezing 25 days a year, on average. Dissipating tropical storms produce strong winds and heavy rains at times.

Austin Care Flite helicopter can, and has, landed on the property for transport to Austin hospitals.

It was evident to us that the residents of The Island enjoy a great deal of camaraderie. A carefree leisure lifestyle predominates.

The Island on Lake Travis, 3404 American Dr., Lago Vista, TX 78645
512/267-7107   800/422-4753

THE OAKS, HENDERSONVILLE, NORTH CAROLINA

Seclusion, Two Miles from Downtown

While attending a seminar at the Center for Creative Retirement at the University of North Carolina at Asheville, we joined a group that toured the town of Hendersonville. It was carnival time, an annual summer celebration on Main Street with food stands, clowns, face decorating for the kids, plus constant local entertainment. All the shops were open for tourists' browsing pleasure. We had a cold drink at the original "old time" drugstore with marble-top counter and iron chairs, which brought back memories.

As we walked the streets, "hellos" and friendliness prevailed. At the Opportunity House, a community recreation center a few blocks down the street, the president greeted us with cookies and cold drinks. She told us that the "House" was twenty-five years old and used to be a

With stained cedar siding, condominiums at The Oaks blend into the natural surroundings.

supermarket. A wing was added to increase the usable space. In some towns this would be called a senior center, but in Hendersonville it attracts two thousand members of all ages at $18 annual dues. The majority are retirees. The Opportunity House kitchen was donated by a local department store, as were many of the woodworking tools. The pottery room was truly a creative enclave. There were rooms for painting, wood carving, weaving, and many other activities. Opportunity House receives no government funds.

Because we were so impressed with the town, we decided to return to see if there was a retirement community in the area that we could include in this book. We found The Oaks.

After coming through a landscaped entrance, we saw small clusters of condominiums at the base of the hillside. There was also a recreation building, along with tennis courts, pitch-and-putt golf practice area, horseshoe and bocci courts.

A drive up the hill and into winding side streets revealed more condos, made of brick and stained cedar siding. The housing clusters blend in with the rock outcroppings, rhododendrons, holly, and hardwood groves. It is evident that great care was exercised to leave as much as possible of the environment in its natural state.

We met resident Janet Duffy, who has lived at The Oaks for three years and helps out in the marketing office. She told us the community is nearly complete, with only a few new units still available. There are two- and three-bedroom units in the complex. A new two-bedroom with loft, two-and-one-half baths, and two decks—about 2,054 square feet—costs approximately $153,000. As a resale it would cost about $145,000. The smallest unit, with 1,490 square feet, is listed at $115,900.

The monthly maintenance fee of $135 includes homeowners' insurance (but does not cover personal property); all outside maintenance of the unit, including painting, cleaning gutters, landscaping, mowing, and snow removal; use of the sports facilities and the clubhouse with an all-weather pool, Jacuzzi, library, and gathering room, lighting and signage; and maintenance of the reserve account. The Oaks has been turned over to the homeowners association and I.P.M. Corp. has been hired to manage the community.

"The majority of the people are retired and it's a great community of caring people," Janet said. Recently she witnessed this firsthand when her husband died after a long illness. The outpouring of assistance and concern from other residents helped carry her through this difficult time. She also appreciates the security she feels in her second-floor condominium.

A community of this size can't afford a social director, so activities are initiated by residents and vary based on the interests of those doing the organizing. To supplement the activities at The Oaks, which may not always suit everyone, the Opportunity House community center proves to be invaluable.

Audrey Reigel, a mutual acquaintance of Janet Duffy and ourselves, is a resident of Hendersonville and an active participant at the Opportunity House. One of her paintings was to be on exhibit at the upcoming art-fest. She told us about the Brevard Music Center in the town of Brevard, twenty-two miles to the west. This Center attracts internationally known musicians, touring Broadway shows, opera, and symphony concerts.

The Oaks' location in Hendersonville (pop. 7,284) is within the city limits, two miles from downtown, one mile from Opportunity House, and one-and-one-half miles from Memorial Hospital.

Hendersonville is in the southwestern part of North Carolina, eighteen miles south of Asheville and fifteen

CLIMATE—1991 TEMP. (°F), PRECIP. (IN.)				OF INTEREST—
	AVG.	MAX.	MIN.	PRECIP.
JAN.	39.2	63	13	3.25
APR.	58.4	82	33	5.38
JULY	75.2	91	59	6.07
OCT.	57.0	80	30	0.19

OF INTEREST—
Total precipitation in 1991 was 43.66 inches. Snowfall in 1991 was 3.5 inches.

miles from the South Carolina border. It is located on a mountain plateau at an elevation of 2,200 feet. The Oaks offers a small neighborhood with built-in neighborliness, involvement in a small active town, and proximity to a large city—an ideal combination for a low-key retirement lifestyle.

The Oaks, P.O. Box 946, Hendersonville, NC 28792
704/697-1008

VILLA TRIESTE, OCEANSIDE, CALIFORNIA

Security with a Breathtaking View

Tucked away on a knoll with views of the Pacific Ocean and the Carlsbad Hills, in the community of Del Oro Hills, is Villa Trieste (VT). Oceanside is midway between Los Angeles and San Diego, along I-5.

Incorporated in 1888, Oceanside has a population of

approximately 130,000 and is forty square miles in area. The beach extends about four miles and features a 1,942-foot municipal fishing pier with a restaurant and lounge located at one end. Overlooking a protected harbor with a large marina capable of berthing fifty-one-foot boats is SeaJet Village, a complex of shops and restaurants.

The developer of this age-restricted community (fifty-five-plus) is UDC Homes, which is listed on the New York Stock Exchange. At build-out in 1994, VT will have 150 condominiums and patio homes.

VT is a gated community with Mediterranean architecture, palm-lined streets, and a recreation center with swimming pool and spa. There are two types of housing. The condominiums are two-story buildings, with a total of sixty-four units. Costs range from $140,990 for a two-bedroom/two-bath, 1,085-square-feet condo to $146,990 for a two-bedroom/two-bath, 1,376-square-feet unit.

Two patio homes are connected and there are 86 individual units. Prices range from $194,990 for a two-bedroom/two-bath with loft, 1,778 square feet, to $205,990 for a two-bedroom/two-bath with loft, 1,849 square feet. Each has a two-car garage.

George Berman, president of the residents association, is a very busy man. The transfer of ownership and control from UDC is progressing. Complicating the matter is the existence of three associations: one for patio homes, another for condominiums, and the master association covering the entire community. He is working to consolidate these.

A retired engineer from Hughes Aircraft, George is

enthusiastic about living at VT. He gave us a sizable list of the features residents like best: The community is four-and-one-half miles from the ocean, with a bus stop out front; there are five major golf courses within five miles, and six nearby tennis courts; a junior college is across the street; a hospital is three miles away, and an enclosed shopping mall is within two miles of VT. Monthly association dues of $145 for patio homes, $167 for condos include a blanket building and earthquake insurance policy.

All activities are run by residents. A recent issue of the monthly newsletter highlighted notes from the last town meeting, a scheduled dinner at an ethnic restaurant, a forthcoming beach party, pool barbecue, handcrafters meeting, a notice of welcome to new residents, review of the van policy and usage, a complaint about the temperature of the pool, and a reminder of the cocktail parties on the third Wednesday of each month at 5:30 P.M.

VT is essentially a neighborhood that has a central meeting/recreational building and a common purpose—you won't find the long list of activity options that the

---

CLIMATE—1991 TEMP. (°F), PRECIP. (IN.)

	AVG.	MAX.	MIN.	PRECIP.
JAN.	57.4	79	42	1.06
APR.	61.7	80	51	0.05
JULY	67.4	76	60	0.24
OCT.	68.0	92	48	0.69

OF INTEREST—
85 percent of the annual rainfall occurs between November and March. The highest temperatures occur in September and October. Snow is rare.

largest RCs offer. The average age is just over sixty-five, and many residents are still employed. Some residents have outside interests associated with their work or within the community of Oceanside. VT is a comparatively small group of neighbors who bond together to form an extended family—a secure feeling in a secure environment.

Villa Trieste, 3340 Sicily Way, Oceanside, CA 92056
619/757-0780

six

MASTER PLANNED COMMUNITIES

What some people see as the advantages of an age-restricted community are disadvantages to others. Many retirees want their children and grandchildren around, and prefer a non-age-restricted master planned community.

Large communities of this type tend to have a variety of housing options suited to residents of different ages, from no age restrictions to areas especially designated for age fifty-five-plus housing, a congregate living complex, or a nursing center.

We have observed that even in communities with no age restrictions, the retirees tend to have their own clubs, interest groups, and sports activities. With common interests and free time, retirees also participate in more community activities than their younger neighbors.

BELLA VISTA VILLAGE, BELLA VISTA, ARKANSAS

Where They Lower the Lakes

"Over there was a valley where I used to ride horses when I was a kid," said Gail Rogers, our corporate office guide at Bella Vista (BV). She was pointing to the middle of a lake, one of the eight man-made lakes at BV. Gail

The country club at Bella Vista Village was designed by internationally acclaimed architect Fay Jones. (PHOTO COURTESY OF COOPER COMMUNITIES, INC.)

grew up in this area of the Ozark Mountains, located in the extreme northwest corner of Arkansas.

As a youngster she knew John A. Cooper during the time he was envisioning what is today a 36,000-acre, 58-square-mile master planned recreation community. Many local residents described Mr. Cooper as "a person who had the vision of a fortune teller and the guts of a gambler." His vision was to develop a planned community and sell homesites to buyers who wanted a holiday/vacation home that in later years would become their retirement haven. BV is the largest of four Cooper Communities.

BV was established in 1965. In June 1993 there were 37,052 property owners and a year-round population of 11,700, about half of whom were retirees. BV is situated thirty-eight miles from the Fayetteville airport and 120 miles from Tulsa International Airport. U.S. 71 runs north and south through the center of the complex, which has golf courses on either side of the highway. At Town Center Shopping Plaza a bridge across the four-lane divided road connects the two sections of the community.

There are no driveways off the main roads, which encircle and crisscross the property. Because of the mountainous topography the roads into the residential areas are winding and branch off into small cul-de-sac communities.

Townhouses start at $60,000, and the most expensive is a lakefront home listed at $500,000. Homesites are sold by Cooper Industries, but buyers can choose their own builder. An architectural control committee reviews house plans for compliance with established guidelines. A local real estate brochure lists resales in a range that can meet most buyers' requirements.

The Property Owners Association (POA) owns the common properties and operates the amenities available to members and guests. Each property owner automatically becomes a member of the POA. The nine-member board of directors is elected by the membership and operates in the same manner as a city council. The general manager works in a capacity similar to a city manager and is appointed by the board. There is a monthly assessment that funds year-round street maintenance and on-call service from three fire departments.

Currently the assessment is $14 a month per property owner, but the Property Owners Association is campaigning to increase the assessment $3 a year for the next three years to a total of $23 a month.

In addition to the monthly fee, residents pay extra for use of various amenities. For example, greens fees for eighteen holes of golf cost $20 for guests or members without an ID card, and $5.25 for members. Swimming, racquetball, and use of exercise equipment costs $2.25 per hour.

COMMUNITY FEATURES

Golf: Four 18-hole, par-72 courses	Tennis: 12 lighted courts
	Fishing: 8 lakes
One executive 18-hole par-63 course	Marina and yacht club
	Library

One 9-hole par-3 walking course	Offices of New York and American stock exchanges
Five recreational centers	18 churches and 2 in the planning stages
Two commerical areas:	
Supermarket	Mildred B. Cooper Chapel
Four banks	Community TV studio
Pharmacy	

Three country clubs, a yacht club, and Kingsdale Grill offer dining and special events such as a Bar-B-Q-Bash with country dancing, as well as Saturday evening dinner dancing.

The BV directory of clubs and civic groups lists over 140 organizations, including one of the largest AARP clubs in the nation. The Bella Vista Village Women's Chorus has appeared on CBS-TV and performed in Washington, D.C.; the Bella Vista Big Band played at President Clinton's Inaugural Ball.

Bates Memorial Hospital is six miles away and ambulance service is provided by a not-for-profit BV ambulance service. On-site is Concordia of Bella Vista Village with twenty catered-living apartments, assisted-living facilities, and skilled nursing.

Retired "Welcome Wagon lady" Margaret Doane is again welcoming newcomers. She and her husband Dick moved to BV five years ago from South Dakota. She oversees a monthly meeting of newcomers and pays particular attention to any problems that come out in the

CLIMATE—1992 TEMP. (°F), PRECIP. (IN.)			OF INTEREST—
	MAX.	MIN.	PRECIP.
JAN.	62	9	1.87
APR.	84	22	.19
JULY	91	61	5.16
OCT.	82	37	.75

OF INTEREST—
Altitude varies from
946 to 1,432 feet.
Total precipitation in
1992 was 48.78
inches.

discussions. She diligently makes sure that every question raised by a newcomer receives an answer.

Dick is an avid golfer, but took time out to build a pier and deck at their lakefront home. He did this when BV lowered the lake level, which happens once a year to allow homeowners to build or repair a pier and clean up the shoreline.

A long lunch with Dick and Margaret helped us understand what it's like to live in a large planned community. Both of them are active and find personal fulfillment in their pursuits. They tried another community in a different state, but feel BV is the best—it meets their expectations and requirements.

Most residents find it refreshing to see younger faces in the recreational facilities, while shopping, and at church. The environment is clean in all respects—a good place to raise children as well as to live the later years to the utmost.

Bella Vista Village, Bella Vista, AR 72714
800/553-6687

BRANDERMILL WOODS, MIDLOTHIAN, VIRGINIA

Five-Step Aging

Living in a rental retirement community with all its support systems, and also having full resident privileges in a 3,500-home planned community, offers the advantages of both a small RC and a large planned community.

The Brandermill planned community is thirteen miles southwest of downtown Richmond, Virginia, and encircles part of the 1,700-acre Brandermill Lake. In 1991 more than two hundred homes were contracted at prices ranging from $60,000 to $450,000. As of mid-1993, only one hundred homesites were still available.

Brandermill residents have access to sailing, fishing, and canoeing; golf at the eighteen-hole course designed by Gary Player; twenty-four tennis courts; five swimming pools; thirty miles of paved trails for walking, jogging, or biking; numerous parks and picnic areas; a community center; and a gardening farm to grow vegetables and trade produce. Some of the above activities require membership in the Country Club. Within the community are medical offices, banks, shopping villages, an inn and conference center, several restaurants, a business park, and four schools. There is easy access to an expressway to

The one-story cluster homes at Brandermill Woods are grouped around cul-de-sacs of two to four units.

Richmond and to major north-south and east-west interstates.

Prior to 1991, Brandermill Woods was a smaller community with fifty-seven cluster homes. Today there is a clubhouse with library, exercise room, beauty/barber shop, card room, craft room, lounge, dining room, and administrative offices. A sixty-bed Health Care Center and an assisted-living facility with sixty studio apartments are five minutes away.

On October 10, 1991, ground was broken for a $12.5 million expansion. Early in 1993, 140 additional cluster homes and club homes were completed. The thirty-acre rectangular plot includes a clubhouse, activity center, and club-home buildings near the center of the complex. The one-story cluster homes are grouped around cul-de-sacs in structures of two, three, and four units. A few units have basements.

CLUB HOMES (apartments) are in two separate three-story buildings that connect into the clubhouse and activity center. The monthly fees, including utilities (except telephone): 1 bedroom, 930 sq. ft., $1,765/ single occupancy, $2,065/double; 2 bedrooms, 1,207 sq. ft., $2,135/single occupancy, $2,435/double. The fee also entitles residents to one meal per day and covered parking.

CLUSTER HOME rental rates, including utilities (except telephone): the smallest, 1 bedroom, 987 sq. ft., $1,550/single occupancy, $1,700/double; the largest, 3 bedrooms, 1,402 sq. ft. (2,792 with basement), $2,620/ single occupancy, $2,770/double. No meals are included. Each home has a covered porch and garage.

ALL RENTAL UNITS have sprinkler systems, burglar alarm, emergency call system, refrigerator, stove, disposal, washer and dryer. Services include exterior and interior maintenance, appliance maintenance, yard maintenance, staff security patrols, and two paid cable TV hookups.

In a discussion with two residents, Mildred Lapsley and Dean Wolfe, we heard only positive comments about

Brandermill Woods. Both participate in bridge, social affairs, and other activities on-site. Dean is president of the Men's Club, which makes him a member of the residents council as well. Both are avid walkers. Mildred participates in the community 150-mile walking club (whose members wear matching caps and T-shirts) and plays golf at the country club. A former teacher and social worker, she now volunteers once a week with "at risk" students in the Brandermill Elementary School. She investigated retirement options in California as well as Virginia, but said that having the medical center nearby was highly influential in her choosing Brandermill Woods.

Dean was a sales engineer with General Electric and lived in Brandermill. When retirement was imminent he scoured both coasts of Florida, but Virginia won out and the Woods met his needs.

An interesting concept emerged from our survey. The monthly BM Woods schedule of events is sparse when compared to those of other retirement communities that are not part of a planned community, but the opportunity to participate in Brandermill activities provides satisfying interaction with a broad spectrum of people of all ages who are not in retirement. It appears that the Woods residents take advantage of these outside activities. The minimum entrance age is fifty-five.

When a retirement community is located in a master planned community, residents have flexibility. In Dean's case, it makes five-step aging possible in one location:

1. Preretirement (a home in Brandermill)
2. Rental cluster home
3. Rental club home
4. The Chesterfield (assisted living)
5. The Health Care Center (nursing care)

CLIMATE—1991 TEMP. (°F), PRECIP. (IN.)					OF INTEREST—
	AVG.	MAX.	MIN.	PRECIP.	Temperatures in
JAN.	40.2	65	16	3.62	December and January reach an average high
APR.	60.2	88	33	0.87	in the upper 40s and
JULY	80.7	99	65	3.47	an average low in the
OCT.	59.9	86	33	2.50	upper 20s. In summer months, temperatures above 100°F are not uncommon.

We find this a commonsense approach to aging in a community that gives residents continuity and lets them maintain the friendships they've developed while getting the care they need.

Brandermill Woods Retirement Community, 14311 Brandermill Woods Trail, Midlothian, VA 23112
804/744-1173   800/552-6579

EDINA PARK PLAZA OF EDINBOROUGH, EDINA, MINNESOTA

The Future Today

From the eighteenth-floor outdoor terrace of Edina Park Plaza retirement community, General Manager Bill Belanger recalled, "This whole area was a big gravel pit, and the 'City Fathers' of Edina decided to develop the pit into a modern business/residential area." Edina is an upscale city southwest of Minneapolis, adjacent to Bloomington, home of the Mall of America.

What evolved is the most innovative complex that we have ever surveyed. Edinborough Leisure Park is the cen-

Edina Park Plaza features an eighteen-story apartment building (left) with roof terraces and a park view.

terpiece. This two-acre city-owned and -operated public park, totally glass-enclosed and kept at a constant 72°F year-round, includes a pool, dressing rooms, walking/running track, ice rink, great hall, waterfall, catering area, children's play area, day care center, and landscaped four-season gardens. Surrounding the park is the retirement community, Hawthorne Suites (Hyatt) Hotel, Corporate Center, and the village homes. Each complex has an entrance into the park.

Edina Park Plaza opened in 1987. There are 202 apartments, 198 currently occupied by 230 residents. The average age is eighty-two. Seventy-five percent of the residents are female and 75 percent are single.

On the first floor of this eighteenth-story building is a private patio facing the park (a great place for people watching), along with a fine arts room, library, mail room, lounge with fireplace, Terrace Club room (for meetings, cards, bingo, and classes), and a large-screen TV. The first floor also has a barber/beauty salon and a restaurant (open daily, 7:00 A.M. to 7:00 P.M.). The entrance from the park and the main entrance are kept locked with access via intercom to the security desk or from the doorman.

On the eighteenth floor are two apartments and outdoor terraces on the east and west corners. There is also a whirlpool and sauna with changing rooms, a fitness center, the Plaza Penthouse for billiards, TV, and cards, and a solarium for seminars, parties, and happy hour.

APARTMENT STYLE	MONTHLY RATE
One bedroom, 623–931 sq. ft.	$1,105–1,710
Two bedrooms, 929–1,200 sq. ft.	$1,503–2,200

The rates above include all utilities (except telephone and cable TV), scheduled transportation on a twenty-two-seat van, weekly housekeeping and towel/linen service, Leisure Park membership, planned activities, and a wellness mini-clinic each week offering health screenings, assessment, and referrals.

Additional services available include breakfast and either lunch or dinner at $225 per month; lunch and dinner, $250 per month; breakfast, lunch, and dinner at $340 per month or à la carte; home care through an affiliate of Fairview Southdale Hospital, with services provided in fifteen-minute increments or up to twenty-four hours a day; and parking in a heated garage for $45 per month.

The monthly activity calendar lists many excursions, happy hours, movies, card games (bridge, poker, "500"), entertainers, classes on various subjects, and a monthly dinner with the manager. In addition, Edinborough Leisure Park sponsors entertainers, a mime showcase, art and clay pot demonstrations, and dances.

Shopping and medical services, including hospitals, are readily accessible. The outer loop (I-494) around Minneapolis–St. Paul is one-half mile away and provides

CLIMATE—1991 TEMP. (°F), PRECIP. (IN.)				OF INTEREST—
	AVG.	MAX.	MIN.	PRECIP.	Blizzards, freezing rain, and tornadoes are common; annual winter snowfall is about 48 inches.
JAN.	12.5	39	−14	0.49	
APR.	49.1	86	22	3.58	
JULY	72.3	94	53	2.95	
OCT.	47.2	79	22	2.52	

ready access to interstate highways and the cultural opportunities of the twin cities.

We talked with Dave Shaich, a resident for six years and a former member of the residents council. His endorsement of the community and how it is run was best described by his longtime friend Floyd Johnson, who said, "Dave is responsible for my being at Edina Park." Floyd became fed up with the regimentation (which included assigned seating at meals) at a nearby community. "Dave showed me the light and I haven't regretted it one bit," he said.

Forward thinking and aggressive action of the Edina city administration could be a model for other cities. Bringing together the segments that make up Edinborough (which keeps retirees in the mainstream) is the future—and it's in the city of Edina today.

Edina Park Plaza of Edinborough, 3330 Edinborough Way, Edina, MN 55435
612/831-4084

FEARRINGTON, FEARRINGTON VILLAGE, NORTH CAROLINA

A Country Village

When we asked directions to Fearrington, we were told, "It's down the road a piece. Look for a small sign and turn right, then right by the cows that have a white belt." Our first surprise was the small sign—a change from the usual billboards that advertise a development. The second surprise was that when we turned by the white-belted cows, we saw no houses under construction. Driving down the road we saw a silo, barn, other farm buildings, a large white farmhouse, cascades of flowers, and a sign that read THE VILLAGE CENTER. This was the hub of Fearrington.

A close friend of ours who was entering retirement told us about Fearrington. He and his wife made an in-depth, on-site survey and were excited about the concept, the facilities, and the residents. The country village environment permeated the development and carried over into the friendliness, enthusiasm, and informality of the many residents who spent time with them. The couple said they immediately felt "at home," and were disappointed when they could not find a house that met their requirements at an affordable price. It was a very difficult decision to pass up Fearrington.

The Camden Park homes at Fearrington face landscaped streets.
(Photo by Bob Donnan)

This master planned community does not have an area designated for retirees; however, 65 to 70 percent of the six hundred families are retired.

Fearrington Farm has been part of the landscape between Chapel Hill and Pittsboro since the 1780s. In 1974 the 1,100-acre farm was sold to Fitch Creations, Inc., run by R. B. and Jenny Fitch. Their dream was to leave the farm structures as originally built, renovate them as required, build additional structures that would blend in with the original buildings, and create the center of a country village. They succeeded.

The original farmhouse is now a restaurant with AAA four-diamond and Mobil four-star ratings. It is also a member of the prestigious Relais & Chateaux, an association of 350 deluxe hotels and gourmet restaurants in thirty-seven countries. Adjacent to the restaurant is a twenty-four-room inn.

We had lunch in what was the granary and is now the market, deli, and café. The former milk barn houses three shops. Other buildings house a bank, bookstore, and more shops. The Center, which resembles a town square, is filled with flowers and bushes, the handiwork of Jenny Fitch.

During the summer, every Tuesday from 4:00 P.M. to dusk a farmer's market operates adjacent to the barn. Seasonal farm products and other items including baked goods, fresh cut flowers, eggs, and goat cheese are offered for sale. All produce must be raised by the farmer and his or her family and sold by a member of the immediate family. All products must be grown or raised within fifty miles of the market. This offers area farmers an opportunity to maintain a place in the local economy.

The barn is an all-weather site for many special events such as dances, pig roasts, and antique and craft shows, and forms the backdrop for many weddings.

The park building, housing a medical center affiliated with the University of North Carolina School of Medicine, was recently completed. Three primary care physicians staff the center. The building also houses a pharmacy, travel agency, architect's office, and a fine craft shop.

On the grounds there is a swim and croquet club, tennis courts, bocci court, and a three thousand-square-foot meeting facility called The Gathering Place. Neighborhoods have been designed to blend into the rolling terrain: some are in the woods, others on what would have been pasture, and each has its own identity.

All building is done by Fitch Creations, Inc. Basic house designs are in keeping with the farm and the rural setting. Single-family homes on one-acre lots start at $190,000; park homes on small lots start at $180,000; connected townhouses start at $175,000. Resales within the fifteen-year-old community start at $120,000.

Homeowners association dues are $65 annually, plus a yearly sewer fee of $100. Townhouse residents pay an additional $110 a month and Camden neighborhood residents pay $65 a month for such services as grounds and exterior maintenance.

Community activities are the responsibility of the "locals," and include an annual Easter Egg Hunt, barn sales, neighborhood block parties, aerobic exercise classes, an investment club, arts and crafts, amateur birders, bocci, men's and women's clubs, and numerous volunteer opportunities. The local merchants also provide unique opportunities: McIntyres Fine Books and Bookends sponsors a summer poetry and music series; Dovecote, a country garden shop, presents garden seminars.

The Village is in Chatham County and is serviced by the County Sheriff's Department and a municipal fire department assisted by volunteers. Chapel Hill city limits is seven miles away, and a supermarket is four miles away.

CLIMATE—1991 TEMP. (°F), PRECIP. (IN.)				OF INTEREST—
	AVG.	MAX.	MIN.	PRECIP.
JAN.	41.9	66	19	4.12
APR.	62.3	86	36	1.04
JULY	80.6	96	67	10.27
OCT.	61.1	84	35	1.40

OF INTEREST— Winter temperatures occasionally drop below 20°F, and snow is a possibility: annual snowfall over the past six years ranged from a trace to twelve inches.

The conveniences of city living are not just around the corner, but neither are the problems associated with city living.

The herd of cows we passed on the way in are Belted Galloway cows, originally from the Highlands of Scotland, and are reported to be the oldest breed of beef cattle. At Fearrington they are community pets, and naming the year's offspring is an annual tradition among the residents.

Another herd of animals lives in a field near the new Camden Park neighborhood. The life-size "Crete" sheep are a new breed—"crete" is short for *concrete!*

As Fearrington develops, R. B. and Jenny Fitch are watching their dream come true. Growth will continue, and completion probably will happen in the year 2010, but according to the Fitches, "It will be planned, gradual growth."

Fearrington, Fearrington Village Center, Fearrington Village, NC 23712
919/542-4000   800/277-0130

FORD'S COLONY, WILLIAMSBURG, VIRGINIA

Colonial Pride

Early in our lengthy conversation with Drew Mulhare, general manager of Ford's Colony, we sensed that this was a different kind of development: he referred to residents as "my clients"!

Drew recounted a recent National Builders Association meeting that distributed large "Off Duty" buttons to attendees. He threw his away. "You're never off duty in this business—always available to a client, and they deserve an honest, straightforward answer to a question or request," he said.

Ford's Colony is located four miles from the center of Colonial Williamsburg, the internationally known restoration of what was the capital city of the Virginia Colony from 1699 to 1780. After sixty years of restoration, Williamsburg now portrays life as it was in Revolutionary days.

The College of William and Mary, chartered in 1693 and the second-oldest college in America, is adjacent to the restoration. The college's Christopher Wren Association for Lifelong Learning offers residents of retirement age opportunities for learning and fellowship through in-depth study, social occasions, field trips, and other activities its membership chooses to sponsor. The special programs office also offers an array of classes from

Ford's Colony in Williamsburg features a forty-five-hole golf course near a nature preserve.   (PHOTO BY JOHN ARRINGTON)

canoeing to painting landscapes to discovering new dance steps.

Ford's Colony is a residential and resort community of 2,500 acres, 250 of which were established as a nature preserve to protect wetlands and habitat. The Colony is marketed to preretirees, who can either purchase a lot for a future retirement home or build immediately and initially use the house as a weekend retreat or vacation home. On completion, the Colony will have 3,250 lots; to date, 1,600 have been sold and 550 homes built. Seventy-five percent of the residents are retired and 25 percent are employed; many commute to Richmond and Norfolk, each fifty minutes away. The developer donated land for a grammar school, and the local high school is less than one-half mile from the entrance to the Colony. The community activity center features a twenty-five-meter pool and all-weather tennis courts. Two more swim and tennis facilities are in the master plan. On the golf courses, thirty-six holes are in use and nine more are under construction. The golf clubhouse covers 23,000 square feet, including an elegant restaurant.

Entrance to the Colony is through controlled gatehouses, and there are constantly roving police patrols. Townhouses range from $185,000 to $260,000; single-family homes from $200,000 to $600,000. The homeowners association owns the twenty-two miles of roads and maintains these through a $650 yearly fee (owners of underdeveloped lots pay $550). Every road is named after a golf course or a legendary hole on a course. It is three miles to a convenience store, five miles to a supermarket, and about fifteen miles to the Patrick Henry International Airport, which is between Williamsburg and Newport News.

Bill and Mary Jane McGrath moved to Ford's Colony in 1986 from Stamford, Connecticut. Their retirement life centers on their family, which includes four children and twelve grandchildren. In between family visits they each play golf twice a week and participate in community activities: Caring Neighbors, a program that provides transportation to medical appointments; Granny's Attic, which loans baby equipment; and Nurse's Corner, which loans medical equipment. They also participate in the Christopher Wren Association at the college. They like having youngsters in the community and avidly support the swim team.

Bill said, "We lucked out by building a small home. A lot of people feel they have to build a big house and then in a few years realize that it's too big for their needs, yet they hesitate to make a move." Mary Jane reflected on a problem they had in choosing a house plan. "Our first choice was turned down by the review committee. They said it was too Victorian, and they were right. The colonial architecture they require is the foundation for the charm of the Colony. We just love it here."

Some changes are forthcoming that will affect the development. General Manager Drew Mulhare told us the developer is about to come to closure with Marriott's time-share division, MORI (Marriott Ownership Resorts, Inc.), to build an upscale time-share complex near the golf clubhouse. He also pointed out a future development

CLIMATE—1991 TEMP. (°F), PRECIP. (IN.)				OF INTEREST—
	AVG.	MAX.	MIN.	PRECIP.
JAN.	43.5	72	19	4.74
APR.	61.6	88	35	6.39
JULY	82.0	100	66	6.46
OCT.	61.9	86	42	4.65

OF INTEREST— Annual snowfall can range from a trace to 24.9 inches.

section of the master plan that may become a retirement community with adjacent health care.

We met many residents at the clubhouse and at a social function and found this to be a buzzing community, filled with young retirees and high energy levels.

Ford's Colony, One Ford's Colony Drive, Williamsburg, VA 23188
800/334-6033

HOT SPRINGS VILLAGE, HOT SPRINGS VILLAGE, ARKANSAS

A Village Near an Old Town

After passing through the gated entrance of Hot Springs Village (HSV) and driving down tree-lined DeSoto Boulevard, we wondered where the people, homes, and stores were. No buildings are visible from the main road, and each homesite adjoins (on one side) either grass and trees, a golf course, or a lake. Not much can be seen by

Lakefront homesites are a favorite in Hot Springs Village, a 26,000-acre community located in the Ouachita Mountains of central Arkansas.
(PHOTO COURTESY OF COOPER COMMUNITIES, INC.)

glancing down the side roads that wind uphill or downhill or curve into the woods.

Turning down a side road brings the houses into view. Each homesite fits into the terrain. There are no swaths cut through the forest with "cookie cutter" homes lined up on each side of the road. Some roads and driveways are very steep, which adds to the uniqueness of the Village. Approximately 5,750 of the 26,014 total acres have been set aside as greenbelt areas.

Construction of HSV started in 1971. The Village is

located in the foothills of the Ouachita Mountains, twenty-two miles north of Hot Springs and sixty miles west of Little Rock. There are approximately 30,000 property owners, and 4,300 homes have been built. About 80 percent of the residents are retired, and 350 students journey to school via five school bus routes.

Loren Summers, who has been employed by Cooper Communities for twenty-three years, was our host. He acts as liaison between the Property Owners Association and the Hot Springs Chamber of Commerce, local schools and boards; he is also responsible for commercial development at HSV. One of his current commercial projects is the Parformance School of Golf, which opened late in 1993. The school is a designed learning and practice facility based around a driving range and three golf holes (two par-four and one par-three), complete with sand traps.

Loren's vast knowledge of Cooper Communities and the inner workings of a large community was invaluable as we tried to understand life at HSV.

Here is a capsule view of the community: *Golf*—five eighteen-hole courses, five pro shops; *Clubs*—two country clubs, four pro shops, restaurants; *Tennis*—eleven lighted courts in two complexes, pro shop; *Swimming*—three pools, one indoor open all year; *Recreation centers*—two, offering a variety of activities; *Lakes*—six, totaling 1,843 acres, marina with boat rental, swimming beach; *Hiking trails*—a thirteen-mile network of walking, wilderness, nature, and fitness trails; *Other*—miniature golf, lawn bowling, basketball courts, softball fields, lake pavilion, two parks, four shopping centers, and fourteen churches. Over one hundred social, civic, and special-interest organizations provide educational, creative, social, and volunteer opportunities for residents.

The Property Owners Association (POA) owns, acquires, builds, operates, and maintains recreational facilities and provides municipal services; determines levies, collects charges and assessments in HSV.

Services provided include police patrols, fire protection with paramedics, 911 call system, and water/sewers; also maintenance of 430 miles of roads, golf courses, recreational areas and facilities, clubs, and restaurants. A committee has architectural control over new residential construction. The association board is elected by the property owners.

Monthly dues for each property owner are $23. In addition, there are user fees. For example: for each property owner, eighteen holes of golf costs $3, or annual unlimited golf, $350; tennis per person, $1.50 for two hours; Natatorium and Fitness Center, $1.75 daily or an annual fee of $185.

Cooper Communities develops some neighborhoods and then sells homes or townhouses. In 1992, 235 new homes were constructed at an average cost of $90,000. The cost of a lot alone ranges from $5,000 to $165,000.

On-site there are doctors' and dentists' offices, and the Good Samaritan Cedar Lodge with eighty-two independent living apartments and an intermediate health care facility. Construction is under way for a thirteen thousand-square-foot medical clinic that will be part of the St. Joseph's Regional Health Care Center located in Hot Springs. AMI National Park Medical Center and two rehabilitation hospitals are also in Hot Springs.

Native Americans used to congregate around the area's forty-seven hot springs, which bubbled from the ground creating vapor clouds. They called this location "The Vapors." Spanish explorers followed, and all of the lakes within HSV are named after them: Balboa, Coronado, DeSoto, and so on.

The lure of bathing in the natural hot mineral waters was the basis for the development of Hot Springs as a celebrated spa. From the late 1800s to the early 1920s, many professional baseball teams came to Hot Springs for their preseason training. Elegant hotels, Bath House Row, ornate buildings, Victorian homes, and the Oaklawn Thoroughbred racing track emerged. A multimillion-dollar renovation of the historic district is under way, and elegance is again on display.

For many years Alice and Roger English journeyed from St. Louis to Hot Springs to enjoy the mineral baths. When it came time for retirement they surveyed California, Arizona, Florida, and South Carolina, but chose HSV in 1989. We met with them in their beautiful lakefront home.

They said they chose this community for several reasons: its proximity to St. Louis, the four-season climate, natural beauty, mostly midwestern population, golf courses, and the large indoor/outdoor swimming pool. Both swim every day, and Alice recently competed in a

CLIMATE—1991 TEMP. (°F)	OF INTEREST—
AVG.	Average annual temperature is 64°
JAN. 43	F; relative humidity, 55 percent;
	total rainfall, 54 inches; snowfall, 4.5
APR. 65	inches. The community is located
JULY 82	slightly southwest of the geographic
OCT. 66	center of the state. It's the eastern
	gateway to the Ouachita Mountains,
	with an altitude of 600 to 800 feet.

swimming event at the National Senior Sports Classic in Baton Rouge, Louisiana.

Roger has taken up golf. Both are active in their church (several churches are on-site). Alice does volunteer work and is editor of the POA newspaper. Her background as a writer for CBS radio and as an occasional freelance writer makes her well qualified for her part-time position. They recalled the pride the community felt when an HSV volunteer group working against adult illiteracy (a major problem in Arkansas) received a Thousand Points of Light Award.

The number of activities available at a community as large as HSV can seem overwhelming, and newcomers must take the initiative: to explore, study, evaluate, and choose according to what will provide personal satisfaction, the foundation for a fulfilling retirement.

Hot Springs Village, Box 970, Hot Springs Village, AR 71902

501/922-0250   800/638-3181

SUN CITY LAS VEGAS AT SUMMERLIN

The Other Las Vegas

One version of Las Vegas is seventy-five thousand hotel and motel rooms, the neon Strip, around-the-clock entertainment, dice clicking on the tables, slot machines ringing, and drive-through wedding chapels.

Another version is the University of Nevada–Las Vegas, the Nevada Symphony Orchestra, Civic Ballet concerts, Senior Theatre U.S.A. Festival, Black History Exhibit, art exhibits—and Sun City Las Vegas (SCLV), eight miles northwest of downtown.

A nine-hole miniature golf course is part of the extensive recreation facilities at Sun City Las Vegas. (PHOTO COURTESY OF DEL WEBB'S SUN CITIES)

Summerlin, Howard Hughes Properties' twenty-five thousand-acre master planned community, is home to SCLV. Twenty percent of Summerlin has been set aside to protect and preserve the natural environment, and eighteen builders have developments under way on the rest. Del Webb was the first to purchase acreage, and SCLV now has 1,892 acres with a mid-1993 population of 5,900 and projected 11,000 population at build-out. Opened in January 1989, this is an age-restricted community: one person in the household must be at least fifty-five, and no one under age nineteen is permitted in permanent residence.

Spring Mountain Range is to the west, Desert National Wildlife Range is north, and Hoover Dam, as well as 550 miles of shoreline in the Lake Mead National Recreation Area, is an hour's drive east.

There are two recreation centers. Mountain Shadows, a $6 million, forty thousand-square-foot center, has a library, 460-seat social hall, multipurpose room, Olympic-size pool, jogging track, tennis courts, racquetball, billiards, bocci ball, exercise room, arts and crafts village, and a nine-hole miniature golf course surrounded by palms and desert landscaping.

Sun Shadows is the second recreation center, with sixteen thousand square feet, which includes an indoor pool with atrium view of the golf course, therapeutic spa, aerobics room, multipurpose room, card room, and juice bar. A contest is under way to determine a name for the third recreation center, still in progress.

Palm Valley Golf Course offers multiple tee placements to accommodate golfers of all skill levels. The par-seventy-two course plays from 5,670 to 6,709 yards.

Highland Falls Golf Course has an elevation of 3,053 feet. The clubhouse opened in March 1993 and is raised above the surrounding areas. The Highlander Restaurant has a separate lounge area with stone fireplace, and floor-to-ceiling windows give diners a view of the mountains, lakes, waterfalls, and golf course.

Ten residents traveled to Baton Rouge, Louisiana, to participate in the U.S. National Senior Sports Organization games in 1993. Our lunch partners, Bill and Margie Kissam, were eligible to make the trip since they were the couples tennis champs in the local Senior Olympics.

The Kissams have lived in Las Vegas for forty years and have always been sports enthusiasts—a contributing factor to their move to SCLV. Many years ago they met as members of the Skating Vanities, a roller skating group that toured the United States and Europe. They finished college during the time their children were also college students. Margie was retiring the day after our lunch from her position as a child development specialist. Bill was in the state legislature for six years, and now is a part-time real estate salesman. Both have a high degree of enthusiasm for the lifestyle they chose.

Forty-four acres at SCLV have been set aside for commercial use, which will include retail stores, banks, medical offices, and financial and legal services. Some stores, financial and professional services, and a post office have been built. Adjacent to the community are many shopping areas, and a major hospital is within a fifteen-minute drive. There are fourteen different model homes: seven single-family homes, four duplex homes, and three attached garden villas. All have two-car garages and covered patios. Single-family and duplex homes have a utility room and an area for a golf cart. Costs include a standard lot. Annual community association dues are $350 per household.

SINGLE-FAMILY HOMES

Elko: 1,171 sq. ft.—2 bedrooms, 2 baths $111,900
Minden: 1,661 sq. ft.—2 bedrooms, 2 baths,
   Nevada room (family room) $153,900
Wendover: 2,564 sq. ft.—3 bedrooms, 2 baths,
   Nevada room $234,900

DUPLEXES

The Individual Ownership/Homeowners Association provides front and rear yard common area exterior landscaping, maintenance is provided by the association for a monthly fee.
Austin: 1,196 sq. ft.—2 bedrooms, 2 baths $110,900
Glenbrook: 1,731 sq. ft.—2 bedrooms, 2 baths,
   breakfast area, Nevada room $163,900

GARDEN VILLAS

Individual Ownership/Homeowners Association provides front and rear yard landscaping; maintenance is provided by the association for a monthly fee.

Charleston: 1,003 sq. ft.—2 bedrooms, 2 baths $89,900
Silver City: 1,279 sq. ft.—2 bedrooms, 2 baths,
   breakfast area $118,900

The community has a total of fifty-two clubs, from crafts, cards, dance, singers, and music makers to aerobics and yoga.

Residents Ron and Zoe Barlow have lived in five large retirement communities. Ron held responsible positions in each community association, including SCLV's. He feels that the association's role is that of watchdog, because at build-out the residents will own the entire community.

The Barlows have been married fifty-nine years. Zoe was a child movie star with Universal Studios prior to Shirley Temple. At SCLV she is president of the computer club, and Ron said whenever anyone in the community has a computer glitch, they say, "Call Zoe." She always helps out, unless she's busy practicing her tap dancing.

The Barlows said that of the retirement communities they've lived in, SCLV was the nicest because "the people are more friendly." Although the Barlows are in their eighties, an age when many people just want to stay put, they said they looked forward to a new environment and new experiences.

CLIMATE—1991 TEMP. (°F), PRECIP. (IN.)				OF INTEREST—
	AVG.	MAX.	MIN.	PRECIP.
JAN.	45.5	71	22	0.21
APR.	64.2	92	43	Trace
JULY	90.2	112	68	0.54
OCT.	72.2	98	36	0.06

OF INTEREST— Mountains of 1,000 to 2,000 feet surround the desert valley. Total precipitation in 1991 was 4.06 inches. Rainy days average 3 per month in winter.

Sun City Las Vegas at Summerlin, 10351 Sun City Blvd., Las Vegas, NV 89134
702/363-5454   800/843-4848

TELLICO VILLAGE, LOUDON, TENNESSEE

Nine Miles Along Tellico Lake

We crossed what seemed like two never-ending dams, then drove a few more miles until we reached the fountain at the entrance to Tellico Village. After a few more miles we finally came upon the lake and civilization. It was beautiful!

Bordering Tellico Lake, which has a surface area of 15,860 acres and a 373-mile shoreline, is 4,592-acre Tellico Village. The terrain varies, from gently sloping to hilly with some rock outcroppings. The highest point is 1,030 feet above sea level and the lowest is 830 feet above sea level.

Tellico Village is located in eastern Tennessee, thirty-one miles southwest of Knoxville and twelve miles south of the intersection of Interstates 40 and 75. Cooper Communities, Inc., founded the community in 1986. There are

With forty miles of shoreline on 15,860-acre Tellico Lake, Tellico Village is ideal for boating and fishing. (PHOTO COURTESY OF COOPER COMMUNITIES, INC.)

a total of 7,000 homesites: 4,500 have been sold, and approximately 600 homes have been built. The village currently has a population of about 1,400.

All lots are within one mile of the water and range in price from $12,000 for a "backwoods" lot to $100,000 or more for waterfront or golf course locations. We drove by large homes that cost half a million dollars, and smaller ones (1,300 square feet) priced closer to $90,000. The homeowner's architect control committee clearly is doing its job, because all homes blend well into the countryside and are compatible with other homes in the many neighborhoods.

The community has a clubhouse and a 6,970-yard golf course. Plans are under way for a new 6,700-yard course to be ready for play in 1997. Overlooking the lake, with a view of the Smoky Mountains in the distance, is the

17,000-square-foot Chota recreation center with meeting rooms, a gym, fitness room, racquetball and tennis courts, and outdoor pool. The center is a hub of activity and is geared to total family participation. The director of the center coordinates many continuing activities and initiates special events such as a white-water rafting trip, whose forty participants ranged in age from sixteen to eighty.

Property owners pay fees to use the various amenities: greens fees, eighteen holes for $4; nine holes, $2; private cart path fee, $200 per year; cart lease per family, $700 per year; pool, fitness room, gym, $1 per day. Tennis and racquetball have separate membership fees.

Located on a peninsula of Tellico Lake is the yacht and country club, the social and cultural center of the village. If features a spacious, well-appointed dining room, cocktail lounge, meeting and card rooms, and a gallery that hosts exhibitions by well-known regional painters and sculptors.

Two resident families invited us to their homes to discuss their experiences and feelings about the village.

"We wanted a location where the winter comes late and spring comes early," said Lydia Bateson, explaining why she and her husband Norm moved to the village. Norm's priority was having a lot on the water where they could have their own dock. They both said they had achieved their goals.

It took only ten minutes to feel that we had known John and Beverly Sullivan all our lives. Four years ago they moved to the Village from the Washington, D.C., area where John was public relations director for the U.S.

Department of Energy and Bev taught school. They are active retirees. Bev is a volunteer teacher at a company that pays its employees to attend a weekly GED course. She also goes to aerobics class three times a week, art class once a week, and is a member of the book club. Last year she and John attended an Elderhostel program in Italy.

John is a true thespian. He organized the Tellico Village Players and played Daddy Warbucks in a recent production of *Annie.* He is an associate editor of *The Hawk,* a monthly newspaper for property owners, and writes a column called "The Village View." He also does some freelance public relations work. His goal is to write a book on retirement in a style similar to that of author and columnist Dave Barry.

The Sullivans are happy with their retirement at Tellico Village. Their only concerns, which they say you have to learn to live with, are the twenty-eight-mile drives to do shopping, the long trip to the airport, and sometimes having to change planes twice to get to your destination.

To help us understand what goes on in the community, John gave us back issues of *The Hawk* from 1993 and copies of his 1992 columns. Some of the highlights:

According to the president of Cooper Industries, Inc., in Tellico Village 96 single-family homes were built in 1992; if the present pace continues there may be 140 new homes in 1993. A commercial center called The Village Square will be built in three phases: ten thousand square feet for the first, seven thousand square feet for the second, and fifteen thousand to twenty thousand square feet for the third. Self-government is the byword of the Prop-

CLIMATE—1991 TEMP. (°F), PRECIP. (IN.)				OF INTEREST—
	AVG.	MAX.	MIN.	PRECIP.	Situated between the Cumberland and Great Smoky Mountains, Tellico receives little snowfall—from 9½ inches in 1989 to a trace in 1991.
JAN.	40	58	14	2.97
APR.	62.8	86	34	3.84
JULY	79.1	94	65	4.06
OCT.	60.7	86	32	1.76

erty Owners Association (POA), of which every property owner automatically becomes a member. The function and responsibility of the POA is to own, lease, acquire, operate, and maintain recreational facilities, roads, and water and sewer systems, and to provide such services as trash collection and fire and police protection. Members pay an assessment of $49.50 per month.

"We say we want to be together," John Sullivan wrote in one of his columns. "We want to be a community, but [sometimes] it seems this togetherness only happens when there is a catastrophe—hurricane, blizzard, flood or a war. But in this community folks have come together as if the flood was coming. It might be because we come to this place from all over the country, that we kind of huddle together and look out for each other. Maybe it's just Tennessee—or maybe the flood is coming."

The catastrophic midwestern flooding of 1993 didn't reach Tennessee, so it must be that the sense of community is the result of a lot of fine folks living at Tellico Village.

Tellico Village, 112 Chota Center, Loudon, TN 37774 800/835-5426

FUTURE

Stonebridge Village, Branson, Missouri

Cooper Communities, Inc., has announced plans to develop Stonebridge Village, a $260 million master planned recreational community, five miles west of Branson, Missouri. The developer has purchased 3,200 acres.

Included will be single-family homes, townhomes, CooperShare Units (time share), and a neighborhood set aside for the celebrity entertainers who choose to live in Branson.

The plan includes a $12 million recreational building and an eighteen-hole championship golf course. Homes will cost from $140,000 to $500,000. By the latter part of 1994, some homes and CooperShare Units will be completed.

Cooper Communities, Inc., Stonebridge Village, P.O. Box 1587, Branson, MO 65616
800/817-8663

Gateway, Fort Myers, Florida

In 1996, Westinghouse Corporation will celebrate the golden anniversary of its entrance into residential and commercial development. During the past five decades they have developed more than fifty-eight thousand acres in the United States.

Gateway is a 5,400-acre master planned community, twelve miles southeast of Fort Myers, which opened in 1989. In early 1993 total residency was 650. There are eight neighborhoods ranging from two- and three-bedroom condominiums on the golf course ($90,000 and up) to single-family houses from $110,000 to $300,000. A 926-student magnet elementary school serves the community, and Florida's tenth public university is projected to open nearby on 850 acres in 1997.

When we surveyed the site in April 1993, it included a thirty-five-acre polo and equestrian center, a private equity membership eighteen-hole golf club, the shell of a medical/dental/health center, a town center market, office park, and two churches. Construction was under way for many other facets of the master plan.

The heart of the community will be "commercial care" serving all of Gateway with hotels, retail stores, restaurants, churches, and offices. The residential communities, comprised of several villages, will blend homes, shops, community facilities, and recreational opportunities into family-oriented living. There will also be a variety of business parks and light industry. Gateway is designed to offer great opportunities to families with children, "empty nest" couples, retirees, and singles. When complete, the community will have twenty-five thousand residents.

Gateway, 11900 Fairway Lakes Dr., Fort Myers, FL 33913
813/561-1000   800/535-0788

COMMUNITIES WITH ADJACENT HEALTH CARE

An apartment, cottage, townhouse, or duplex in a retirement community that provides meals and activities gives retirees the opportunity to reduce the responsibilities of home ownership, including housekeeping, maintenance, and yard work, while maintaining independence. The advantage of congregate living is that residents are not alone, as is often the case if they were to rent an apartment in a large complex. Unfortunately, old-time neighborliness just doesn't happen very often.

Built-in opportunities for interaction through community interest groups, clubs, and educational programs are a distinct advantage. From these social activities, residents develop a support group—a form of extended family—that gives them a feeling of acceptance and security. As residents age and health problems develop, this "comfort" becomes invaluable. Living in a community with health care on-site allows them to keep their extended family intact.

This chapter includes communities with home care, assisted living, and intermediate and skilled nursing care.

BERMUDA VILLAGE, ADVANCE, NORTH CAROLINA

At Bermuda Run Country Club

Included in the price of a condominium or villa at Bermuda Village (BV) is a full membership in Bermuda Run Country Club, home of the Bing Crosby Celebrity Golf Tournament, which attracts hundreds of spectators and many celebrities each year. We first surveyed BV in mid-1992 while preparations for the tournament were under way.

BV is ten miles west of Winston-Salem (population 143,485 in 1990), which offers many services, educational and cultural resources, including the North Carolina School of the Arts, part of the University of North Carolina system; Bowman Gray School of Medicine, part of Wake Forest University; Forsyth Memorial Hospital; and the Piedmont Triad International Airport, near Greensboro.

During our first survey we were told that a skilled nursing facility would be added to the personal care/assisted living medical center, which also houses a satellite clinic operated by Bowman Gray School of Medicine.

The focal point of Bermuda Village is its 30,000-square-foot clubhouse.

When we learned that the addition was complete, we added BV to our 1993 survey list.

BV is a privately owned 225-resident retirement community located on fifty acres within the Bermuda Run Country Club. There is a separate large residential area built along the fairways of the twenty-seven holes of golf. Both entryways to the club are gated and staffed.

The focal point of the village is the thirty thousand-square-foot clubhouse, which includes a concierge, front desk security, administrative offices, the On-the-Rocks Pub, a fireside lounge, TV room, billiards, Ping-Pong, a library, beauty/barber shop, art studio, apothecary shop, sauna and steam room, indoor swimming pool, whirlpool, exercise room and health center, outdoor terraces, a woodworking shop, residents' gardens, and a multitude of scheduled activities.

All villas and condo units are purchased by residents. If a resident leaves, BV buys back the property. Two T-shaped multistory condominium buildings branch off from the clubhouse. Heated and air-conditioned passageways cross a large pond and provide entry to the condos. There is valet parking, and a golf cart transports residents from the clubhouse entryway to individual units.

Villas, mostly duplexes with some singles, are built in neighborhood style on curving roads. Most neighborhoods have about eighteen units. The fifth phase of the villa development was announced in 1993.

COSTS

Villa/1 bedroom, 1 bath, carport, 1,090 sq. ft. $185,500
Villa/2 bedrooms, 2 baths, carport, 1,245 sq. ft. $199,500

All condos are resale and range from $127,500 for a one-bedroom to over $200,000 for a deluxe two-bedroom, two-bath with study.

Monthly service fees for villas and condos range from $1,200 to over $2,000 a month. This includes $90 per month per person for dining credit, weekly housekeeping, laundry of linens and flat laundry, yard/exterior maintenance, and use of all facilities at BV.

A $5,000 health center deposit entitles each resident to sixty-five nights in any level of care at the center. Any unused portion of the deposit is refundable upon departure or death.

All facilities of the Bermuda Run Country Club are also available to residents; a $20 per month minimum food purchase is required.

During our first survey we visited with Weaver and Louise Hatcher in their villa and then had dinner in the club dining room. The Hatchers moved to BV during its early stages in 1985, after retiring in 1978 and selling their jewelry store in Fayetteville, North Carolina. The furnishings of their two-bedroom villa reflects a lifestyle of southern gentleness, and they are very pleased with life at BV. Weaver plays golf, tennis, and Ping-Pong. Louise spends considerable time volunteering at the health center, and also teaches a Bible class.

Following dinner we toured the surrounding area and ended up at nearby Tanglewood, another tremendous asset to living at BV. This 1,152-acre farm was given to Forsyth County by the Reynolds family in 1951, and is now a fabulous park that includes two golf courses: the Championship Course, where the Vantage Championship of the Senior PGA Tour takes place each year, and a par-three course. A redesigned barn for group gatherings holds seven hundred people. In addition, there is a clubhouse; the Reynoldses' home, which is now a bed-and-breakfast inn; the Mount Pleasant Church, which first opened in 1809; major horse shows, five steeplechase races, and much more.

On our latest visit we chatted with a group having mid-morning coffee, including two sisters, one of whom

CLIMATE—1991 TEMP. (°F), PRECIP. (IN.)				OF INTEREST—
	AVG.	MAX.	MIN.	PRECIP.
JAN.	40.8	64	18	4.53
APR.	60.7	84	33	6.66
JULY	79.5	97	64	3.95
OCT.	60.3	84	34	1.90

OF INTEREST—
Total precipitation in 1991 was 41.8 inches. Annual snowfall ranges from a trace to 24 inches. Some hail is reported each year.

had just moved to BV after living in Hawaii for twenty-eight years. She wanted to be near her sister, and finds this lifestyle very fulfilling. These folks were "happy campers."

This is a friendly, upscale community and could definitely be considered a golfer's paradise.

Bermuda Village, P.O. Box BVI, Advance, NC 27006
919/998-6535   800/843-5433

BRISTOL VILLAGE, WAVERLY, OHIO

Homey

"We don't have an activity director," said Leona Rafferty, president of the Bristol Village residents association. "Everything that goes on here is initiated by residents and carried through by residents."

This was how our roundtable discussion with seven residents began. The thirty-one-year old village is a not-for-profit community affiliated with National Church Res-

Bristol Village has nearly 400 single-family homes.   (PHOTO BY ROB EBERST)

idences (NCR), headquartered in Columbus, Ohio. The NCR mission statement, in part, "is to provide housing and care and to promote active independence in retirement at affordable prices in communities of caring persons. Our ministry is national in scope and originates from a Christian commitment of service to older adults and the handicapped." There are 140 NCR facilities throughout the United States.

We discussed the 133-acre village from the residents' point of view. Unique to this meeting was the presence of Jay and Barbara Early, executive director and office manager respectively, who are also residents. This was the first time we had visited a community whose director lived on-site.

Leona told us that Bristol Village has nine standing

committees: arts and crafts, development (where all new ideas are channeled for action), enrichment hour (a stimulating discussion topic each Thursday evening), financial, health center and assisted living, safety, swimming pool center, welcome, and worship. The chairpersons of these committees make up the executive committee of the association.

Special committees are formed for events such as the Thanksgiving and Christmas dinners, an Independence Day bicycle parade, block parties, and so on.

The twenty-page March 1993 issue of *Bugle,* the monthly publication of the community, featured announcements of geriatric thespians' tryouts, a new computer center, an international relations group meeting, a theological forum, singles' luncheon, women's news, town meeting, financial and estate planning seminar, garden news, and the village bus schedule. Forty-eight regular activities also were listed. BV is a busy place.

A retired minister and his wife were part of our discussion group. They said BV's financial arrangements were a lifesaver for them. Because they had always lived in a parsonage provided as part of each ministerial assignment, they would have had difficulty managing a down payment and paying off a substantial mortgage. Residents have a choice of three financial plans, and one fit this couple's need for affordable housing. They mentioned that thirty-nine other ministers also live in the village.

Bristol Village is located in the small town of Waverly in southern Ohio, sixty miles south of the capital city of

Columbus and the Port Columbus International Airport. It is thirty miles north of Portsmouth, Ohio.

BV has 397 single-family homes, an activity center, fitness center with indoor heated pool and spa, 82 assisted-living apartments, and a 50-bed fully licensed skilled and intermediate nursing facility that is Medicare- and Medicaid-approved. The community is AAHA Continuing Care Accredited.

FINANCIAL ARRANGEMENTS

An entrance contribution of $1,000 per person reserves a house.

Entry Fee—Three Options:

1. *Life use plan*—Refundable during first fifty months, minus 10 percent administration fee and 2 percent of the balance for each month of residency. No restrictions on reason for leaving.
2. *Capital recovery plan*—85 percent of entry fee refundable upon reoccupancy of house.
3. *Monthly payment plan* (rental)—Obligated for first twelve monthly payments, then leave with sixty days notice.

MONTHLY MEMBERSHIP FEE: Includes exterior home maintenance, lawn fertilizing, tree trimming maintenance of sidewalk and driveway, building insurance, cable TV, use and upkeep of all common areas, and property taxes.

STANDARD RENOVATION: Each home includes choice of carpeting, new kitchen cabinets and countertops, new tub and shower units, interior painting, central air-conditioning, exterior vinyl siding, lawn renovation and landscape package, and new overhead light fixtures.

COST EXAMPLE: 2 bedrooms, 2 baths, living room, family room, carport:

1. *Life use*—Fee $72,100. Monthly fee, single $382.50, double $393.
2. *Capital recovery plan*—Fee $125,400. Monthly fee, single $382.50, double $393.
3. *Monthly payment plan*—$980, plus extended home warranty $54, and single $382.50, double $393.

Assisted living and skilled nursing fees are additional.

Residents of the village are from all walks and levels of life, from around the United States and some foreign countries. Residents report a high level of compatibility—the community averages one wedding every eighteen months!

Residents also show a tremendous sense of cooperation and loyalty to their neighbors. This is best illustrated by two very confidential resident-administered "aid" funds—one is for continuing assistance when the going gets tough, and the other is a one-time, as-needed, short-term "helping" package.

CLIMATE: Southern Ohio's Pike County, which includes Waverly, is temperate with few extremes. Average July temperature is 70°F or higher; January temperatures average 30 to 40°F. Precipitation averages about 40 inches annually, concentrated in the spring, summer, and fall. There are about 175 frost-free days (May through October).

Bristol Village, 111 Wendy Lane, Waverly, OH 45690
800/223-9766

PATRIOT HEIGHTS, SAN ANTONIO, TEXAS

Success After Adversity

Although Patriot Heights is surrounded by nine hospitals within a one-mile radius, open fields surround the community itself. Most of the vacant land is owned by medical foundations, and the general area is known as the Medical Center Complex in northwest San Antonio.

We made our first visit to this community in the late 1980s, when it was called The Village on the Heights. At that time we were impressed with the facility and the location, but the management was in transition and residents were uneasy about the changes.

Since that time, the original developer declared bankruptcy and NBA Ventures Company, a wholly owned, for-profit subsidiary of the National Benevolent Association of the Christian Church (Disciples of Christ),

Some apartments at Patriot Heights look down into this atrium where social activities and programs make full use of the open space.

(PHOTO COURTESY OF PATRIOT HEIGHTS)

became involved. On December 31, 1991, the National Benevolent Association officially acquired the facility from NBA Ventures Company.

NBA was officially chartered on March 10, 1887. Today there are seventy NBA-related facilities throughout the United States. More than nine thousand persons live in NBA facilities, and the total ministry reaches more than twenty-seven thousand individuals annually with direct services. Their motto is very simple: "What we do best is care."

We made our second visit in September 1993 and found the community 100 percent occupied with 254 residents, and a waiting list of 50 people. We talked with a resident who had been there since the beginning.

Mary Jane Clark and her husband Kenneth were among the very first residents at what is now Patriot Heights. Before retirement they lived in Wisconsin, where Mary Jane was a social worker of national renown. She has recently completed a six-year governor's appointment to the Texas Planning Council for Development of the Disabled.

Mary Jane discussed in detail the problems of the previous managements. The original developers were inexperienced in RC operations, and did not know how to market the facility. As deficits increased, services decreased, which caused resident resentment and created an "us versus them" environment. The current owners are pros in the field. She assured us that the community, under the guidance of the NBA, is now excellent—"It's a wonderful place to live."

The medical center is being expanded and modernized, a new van has been purchased, and the on-site management is effective and caring. We appreciated her candor and feel all is well at Patriot Heights.

MONTHLY RENTAL FEES—5 apartment styles and 4 villa styles available:

Apartment—Studio, 490 sq. ft.	$765
2 bedrooms/2 baths, 975 sq. ft.	$1,400 single
	$1,750 double
Villa—1 bedroom/bath/studio, 1,050 sq. ft.	
	$1,430 single,
	$1,780 double
2 bedrooms/bath/atrium, 1,520 sq. ft.	$1,795 single,
	$2,145 double

Costs include one meal per day per person plus continental breakfast; housekeeping service every two weeks; utilities (except telephone and cable TV); maintenance; transportation; wellness clinic; linen service (for apartments only); in-home care; covered parking; and twenty-four hour manned security.

Amenities of the complex include an emergency call system, full-time social director, chapel, beauty/barber shop, heated swimming pool, private dining room, whirlpool, exercise room, library, country store with ice cream parlor, arts and crafts room, meeting rooms, a lounge, and a full monthly calendar, which includes happy hour.

As we waited to see the executive director, Maria de Lourdes Zendejas, a resident in a wheelchair introduced herself and welcomed us to the community. A friendly

CLIMATE—1991 TEMP. (°F), PRECIP. (IN.)

	AVG.	MAX.	MIN.	PRECIP.
JAN.	48.9	81	30	5.08
APR.	72.4	90	42	4.91
JULY	84.5	103	71	2.23
OCT.	73.3	99	39	0.87

OF INTEREST—
Total precipitation in 1991 was 42.76. Summer temperatures are above 90°F about 80 percent of the time. The temperature drops below 32°F about 20 days a year.

conversation took place, and she was obviously very upbeat about the community. Maria arrived, joined the conversation, and on leaving for her office gave the resident a hug. The NBA motto came once more to mind: "What we do best is care."

Patriot Heights, 5000 Fawn Meadow, San Antonio, TX 78240
512/696-6005

ROLLING GREEN VILLAGE, GREENVILLE, SOUTH CAROLINA

Homespun

Rolling Green Village (RGV) is located on 170 acres of rolling terrain that was once the dairy farm of Hoke and Mildred Smith. The Smiths made a gift of the land to the

Rolling Green Village provides active living, companionship, and security in a Christian environment. (PHOTO BY M. LYNN MCQUEEN)

Greenville Baptist Retirement Community Board of Trustees. Now the farm has winding roads that lead to 163 homes, 110 apartments, 28 personal care apartments, and the Mildred Smith forty-four-bed health care facility. Mrs. Smith still lives nearby in a red brick ranch house.

RGV is neither controlled nor financially supported by the South Carolina or Southern Baptist Conventions. The Greenville Baptist Retirement Board of Trustees is a local group of Christian business and religious leaders established by the Greenville Baptist Association. Their sole mission is to establish and maintain a place of residence for retired persons. Parkside Senior Services manages RGV.

"Cast me not off in the time of old age; forsake me not when my strength faileth." Psalms 71:9.

According to RGV literature, this passage of scripture serves as the focal point for the purpose and philosophy of the community. Residence at RGV is available to anyone who has the desire for active living, companionship, and security in a comfortable Christian environment.

In the northwest corner of South Carolina, RGV is located fifteen minutes from downtown Greenville and thirty minutes from Spartanburg. The recently renovated Greenville-Spartanburg Regional Airport is four miles away and is serviced by American, Delta, and US Air. Two shopping malls are within six miles of the community. There are two hospitals in town and an emergency care center less than two miles away.

Greenville has a population of 58,282 (1990) and is known as the "Textile Center of the South." The "big news," however, is that BMW has announced plans to build a plant in town. There are five colleges and universities in the area, including Furman University, founded in 1826, and Bob Jones University.

Cultural opportunities include a concert association, Greenville ballet, chorale, concert band, symphony, chamber players, Theater on the Green (celebrating its twenty-fifth anniversary), and activities at the colleges.

Around the perimeter of the village are two retirement neighborhoods. Homes within each neighborhood are purchased on a "fee simple" basis: the quoted price is for a basic home and lot. On the following page are two unit types, cost, and monthly fee.

At RGV, a person can purchase a home and participate in any community activities as desired. If medical problems or infirmities develop, the resident can sell the home and move to the apartments, which provide one meal, housekeeping, and other services. NOTE: Another cost program that involves a modest refundable entry fee and monthly fee is available for residents who need to move to the personal care unit and then to nursing care if necessary.

We had a long talk with the head of security, Tommy Henderson, who has worked at the village since it opened in 1987. His duties involve participation in difficult situations such as medical emergencies, as well as the routine business of keeping the community secure. His comments were heartfelt, and when he said, "It's a great place," he backed it up with many examples. He drew our attention to a chart in the foyer showing the residents' contributions toward the purchase of a van. He also told us that the residents contributed funds toward completion of the master landscaping plan.

The community is neat, well maintained, and highly functional, but not plush. Residents agree that a caring community doesn't have to be elegant. We read the chart announcing the fund-raising campaign for a forty-eight-passenger bus: $48,000 was needed and $32,000 had been pledged. That's community spirit!

When we first drove around the community we ad-

HILLSIDE NEIGHBORHOOD

CHOICE OF LOT LOCATION	FEE SIMPLE PURCHASE PRICE	MONTHLY FEE
2 bedroom duplex, 1,200 sq. ft.	$88,100	$159.00*
3 bedroom cottage, 1,590 sq. ft.	99,550	159.00*

MORNINGSIDE NEIGHBORHOOD

CHOICE OF LOT LOCATION	FEE SIMPLE PURCHASE PRICE	MONTHLY FEE
2 bedroom duplex, 1,200 sq. ft.	$ 90,250	$149.00**
3 bedroom cottage, 1,650 sq. ft.	108,250	149.00**

*Includes a $94 basic monthly fee that covers village staff; access to intermediate/skilled nursing care facility; routine health checks; twenty-four-hour emergency call system; security; scheduled transportation; special trips, events, programs, and activities sponsored jointly by management and the residents association. The $65 homeowners association fee covers grounds maintenance around homes and common areas; exterior maintenance and repair of individual homes; trash removal; street lighting; message service at reception desk; and hazard insurance on home.

**Includes $55 homeowners association fee, which covers all of the above *except* grounds maintenance around homes and within common areas.

A resident membership fee of $3,000 per person is applicable to all units at RGV. Units may be resold to any other qualified community member at any time.

CLIMATE—1991 TEMP. (°F), PRECIP. (IN.)				OF INTEREST—
	AVG.	MAX.	MIN.	PRECIP.
JAN.	41.8	63	18	4.72
APR.	62.1	85	35	5.65
JULY	80.5	97	67	5.75
OCT.	61.6	86	35	0.24

OF INTEREST— Total precipitation in 1991 was 47.25 inches. Elevation is from 800 to 1,100 feet. Winter often includes two freezing rains and two to three small snowstorms.

mired the landscaping, three lakes, and Canada geese. The attractive four-by-four-foot flowering planter boxes covering all of the street drainage sewers left a lasting impression with us. It's homespun.

Rolling Green Village, 1 Hoke Smith Blvd., Greenville, SC 29615
803/297-0558

THE BROADWAY PLAZA, FORT WORTH, TEXAS

At Cityview

When we moved to Dallas in 1970 we were told about "Cowtown," that other city thirty miles to the west officially known as Fort Worth. For decades there was much rancor between residents of Cowtown and those of "Big D." This disappeared in 1973 when Dallas–Fort Worth International Airport was built between the two cities and the entire area became known as the Metroplex.

Fort Worth has a population of about 448,000, and according to the *Texas Almanac,* the Dallas–Fort Worth area has the ninth-largest population of U.S. metropolitan areas: 3,885,415.

Today, "Cowtown" refers to the ninety-eight-acre Fort Worth Stockyards National Historic Area. Other area attractions include a 100,000-square-foot Billy Bob's Texas, billed as the world's largest honky-tonk, as well as a cultural district two miles west of downtown with the Casa Mañana Theatre, Kimball Art Museum, Modern Art Museum, Amon G. Carter Museum, and Museum of Science and History, noted for its Planetarium and Omni Theater.

About seven miles southwest of downtown, in an expanding area known as Cityview, is Broadway Plaza. The RC is built on a knoll that offers views of the Fort Worth skyline on one side, cattle ranges on another.

This is a full-service gated rental community that opened in December 1987 and is built on twenty-two acres. There are 82 apartments, 77 villas, and a health center with assisted living (40 beds), intermediate and skilled nursing care (total 121 beds). Within a two-mile radius are three hospitals, a physicians' medical center, and numerous shopping areas. The airport is forty-five minutes away.

The American Retirement Corporation purchased this complex from Forum Group, Inc., on April 1, 1992. ARC was founded in 1978 and is focused exclusively on retirement housing. The community is 92 percent occupied (94 percent reserved) with an average age of eighty.

The Broadway Plaza is a twenty-two-acre rental community with apartments, villas, and a health center that offers several levels of care.

COSTS

Apartments (4 models), single occupancy; for second person, add $445

Alcove Studio (600 sq. ft.):	$1,400–1,675
1 bedroom, 1 bath (716 sq. ft.):	$1,750–1,950
2 bedrooms, 2 baths (1,081 sq. ft.):	$2,100–2,400
2 bedrooms, 2 baths (1,322 sq. ft.):	$2,350–2,995

Villas (3 models), single occupancy; for second person, add $445

1 bedroom, 1½ bath, den (997 sq. ft.):	$1,590–1,990
2 bedrooms, 2 baths (1,124 sq. ft.):	$1,890–2,440
2 bedrooms, 2 baths, den (1,303 sq. ft.):	$2,440–2,840

As in most RCs, the apartments and villas include a fully equipped all-electric kitchen, washer and dryer, wall-to-wall carpeting, smoke detectors, emergency alert system, safety bars in tubs and showers, basic cable TV service, telephone jacks, individual temperature controls, reserved parking for apartment residents, and garages for villa residents.

Services include twenty-eight to thirty-one meals a month, plus continental breakfast; utilities (except telephone); weekly housekeeping and flat linen service; all interior/exterior maintenance and landscaping; and transportation. Each resident is entitled to fifteen days per year free use of the health center (maximum sixty days/lifetime).

A full-time activity director coordinates a fully scheduled monthly activity program. Residents have free use of a library, billiards room, greenhouse, card rooms, indoor swimming pool, wellness and exercise programs, arts and crafts studio, elegant conversation nooks and parlors, Danes Place (a lounge for happy hour—snacks provided, bring your own beverage), banking services offered once a week, gift shop open twice a week, and beauty/barber shop.

NOTE: An optional fee plan for villa residents, known as Standard Service Plan, includes all of the above *except* transportation, electricity, cable TV, meals, and housekeeping. Monthly fee schedules for single occupancy as follows: 997 sq. ft., $1,100 to $1,490; 1,124 sq. ft., $1,390 to $2,290; 1,303 sq. ft., $1,890 to $2,290. For a second person, add $125.

CLIMATE—1991 TEMP. (°F), PRECIP. (IN.)				OF INTEREST—
	AVG.	MAX.	MIN.	PRECIP.
JAN.	42.8	72	23	2.72
APR.	67.4	93	42	3.63
JULY	85.0	101	67	3.99
OCT.	68.1	97	34	9.32

OF INTEREST— Winters are mild; northers (storms) occur about three times each month, accompanied by sudden drops in temperature.

We talked with Polly Booth, president of the residents association and a resident for four years. She lived in Fort Worth, and when her husband died she made the move to one of the villas. "It's a great place," she said. "High standards, very secure, interesting new friends—I'm very happy here." Polly feels the new owners know what they are doing and the new on-site management is great to work with.

Broadway Plaza is an upscale RC. It is well maintained and in an excellent location. Security is exceptional: there's a manned, gated entrance, and the head of security lives in the community. The medical center has large rooms with lounge areas for family get-togethers, and an alcove off the dining room for family or special-occasion dinners. Those who want a modern RC in a progressive city, with just a bit of Cowtown, may want to consider the Broadway Plaza at Cityview.

The Broadway Plaza, 5301 Bryant Irvin Rd., Fort Worth, TX 76132
817/294-2280

FUTURE

Lake Pointe Landing, Hendersonville, North Carolina

Groundbreaking ceremonies took place June 3, 1993, at the thirty-two-acre complex in northeast Hendersonville. Future residents of this community will purchase patio homes that are built in pods of four to six units. The first residents are expected to arrive in the spring of 1994, with build-out expected in 1997.

There are three styles of homes: 2 bedrooms, 1 bath (1,637 square feet), $141,000; 2 bedrooms, 2 baths (1,773 sqaure feet), $159,000; 2 bedrooms, 2 baths, and den (1,995 square feet), $178,500.

Each unit has a loft and garage. Units with basements and for prime locations cost extra. The monthly service fee is $595, plus $185 for the second person. This covers exterior maintenance, property insurance, long-term care insurance (eighty-bed nursing facility on-site), and use of the clubhouse. There will be a full-time activity director.

Title to the home is "fee simple," but there is a restriction: on resale, the buyer must be over fifty-five years of age. At build-out the developer will continue to manage the complex, with residents in an advisory role. The site is located within two miles of I-26, and there is abundant shopping in the area.

Lake Pointe Landing, 420 Thompson St., Hendersonville, NC 28739
704/693-7800

The Highlands, Pittsford, New York

Located along the 363-mile Erie Canal, ten miles southeast of Rochester, New York, is the town of Pittsford. The one-block downtown area is supplemented by interesting shops and restaurants in historic buildings bordering the canal.

The Highlands, a not-for-profit senior living community consisting of 96 independent-living apartments, 48 enriched-housing units (assisted living), and a 122-bed nursing facility, will be built on 52 acres within walking distance of downtown Pittsford.

Completion is expected in November of 1994. Highland Hospital of Rochester is the sponsor, and Greystone Communities, Inc., will build and manage the community.

Greystone Communities, Inc., 222 W. Las Colinas Blvd., Irving, TX 75016
214/402-3700

eight

LIFE-CARE COMMUNITIES

The only significant difference between life-care communities and communities with adjacent health care is in the financial arrangements. Instead of billing residents for health services as needed, life-care communities require payment up front in addition to the usual monthly fee. This is a prepayment of care for life, including all levels of nursing care.

The concept is appealing because it provides residents with a sense of total security, but the arrangements are complicated. If you're considering a life-care financial situation, you'll need to study the financial condition of the RC in depth. There is no uniformity among communities in benefits that are included. Each is unique, so comparisons are difficult. This lifestyle involves the commitment of a great deal of money.

One source of information for evaluating the operating effectiveness and financial condition of a life-care RC is the American Association of Homes for the Aging (AAHA), which has established a Continuing Care Accreditation Commission.

An RC that seeks voluntary AAHA accreditation devotes at least a year to self-analysis of *all* aspects of the RC. Resident study groups assist in the preparation of the self-evaluation. The RC's report is then submitted to the commission, which asks for clarification and further analysis if necessary. If all goes well, an accreditation team spends many days on-site probing and comparing the actual operation to the self-analysis that the RC prepared.

RC executive directors who have gone through the accreditation process say it is a grueling experience, but they have found the self-analysis very worthwhile. The on-site inspection teams include executive directors of other RCs who know what questions to ask and where to look.

It should be understood that the fact that an RC is not accredited does not mean it is inferior. There are many classifications of RCs included in the commission's definition of eligible RCs. AAHA does not restrict the process to life-care communities. There are over 160 accredited communities nationwide.

CAROLINA MEADOWS, CHAPEL HILL, NORTH CAROLINA

In a Setting of Southern Tradition and Culture

Upon entering the recreation building at Carolina Meadows (CM) we were immediately drawn to a long corridor of Sheetrock that was covered with cartoon drawings of life at this community. A major expansion was under way to double the size of the building. One wall had been torn down and replaced with the temporary Sheetrock wall, which included a built-in window for the "sidewalk superintendents."

The colorful lobby mural was created by resident Betty McMahan. Later, as we toured the facility, we met up with this talented artist and found her a tremendous booster of CM. She mentioned that the local evening news that day would feature a human-interest segment featuring "the wall." The residents' monthly publication, *The Meadowlark,* always contains many of Betty's drawings, each one a humorous illustration of one segment of an article.

Located in the country, yet less than five miles from the center of Chapel Hill, CM's 160 acres blend into the wooded rolling countryside. This non-profit community is being developed in three phases.

Phases One and Two are completed, and Phase Three is in progress. Currently there are 380 residents living in 267 apartments and villas: 140 men, 28 of whom are

Carolina Meadows' 160 acres blend into the rolling wooded countryside.

single, and 240 women, of whom 128 are single. The average age is seventy-nine, although residents range in age from sixty-one to ninety-seven. When the community is completed in 1995, there will be a total population of about 600 residents.

The addition to the recreation building includes a 265-person dining room and a private dining room for up to 40 diners. The auditorium has a raised platform and dance floor. An addition of 40 beds to the health center, and construction of an assisted living complex, is scheduled for completion in 1995.

Each of the three phases has a three-hole, par-three golf course; these eventually will be converted into one continuous nine-hole course. Amenities include walking and bicycle trails, garden spaces, enclosed swimming pool, health spa and Jacuzzi, tennis courts, bocci, shuffleboard, croquet and horseshoe courts, craft room, woodworking shop, beauty/barber shop, billiards, meeting rooms, and a lounge adjacent to the dining room with individual lockers for storage of personal beverage choices.

Financial arrangements are referred to as the Equity Concept. There are four villa models, which range in price from $148,500 to $197,500, and seven apartment models that range from $74,700 to $179,000. The amount applicable to the unit chosen is paid at sign-up and is 100 percent refundable whenever the unit is vacated for any reason; the refund is paid to the resident's estate in the event of death.

For example, one hundred villas will be built in Phase Three. The payment for each villa is the cost of the building. When a resident leaves and collects his refunded payment, a new resident moves in and pays the full amount of the unit cost. The Equity Concept plan will result in little or no long-term debt when the project is completed, which will result in lower monthly service fees.

As stated earlier, this is a non-profit organization, and one-third of the board of directors must be residents. The board determines the monthly service charge. In 1993 it was $950 single occupancy, $1,225 double occupancy, which included a $125 monthly meal allowance per person.

All residents pay for their own utilities. The monthly service charge covers prorated property taxes, an emergency call system, grounds care, building maintenance and insurance, security, water and sewer service, trash removal, utilities for the common areas, scheduled transportation and programs, cable TV, use of common facilities, and administrative costs. If a resident wants housekeeping, laundry, or any other personal services, CM will provide them for an additional fee.

All health care costs are the individual's responsibility. Residents must have health insurance. A Life Care Reserve Fee of $5,000 for a single and $7,500 for a double is paid at sign-up and is nonrefundable. The accumulation of these funds results in a large reserve that is used to pay for medical costs of residents who have depleted their own funds. This is the basis of the stated policy that no resident will be required to leave because of an inability to pay. This community is AAHA Continuing Care Accredited.

CLIMATE—1991 TEMP. (°F), PRECIP. (IN.)				OF INTEREST—
	AVG.	MAX.	MIN.	PRECIP.	Winter weather usually
JAN.	41.9	66	19	4.12	includes some snow and sleet, but
APR.	62.3	86	36	1.04	excessive accumulation
JULY	80.6	96	67	10.27	is rare.
OCT.	61.1	84	35	1.40	

We were given a Table of Organization of the residents association to help us understand how this association functions. At the top is the council, made up of a five-member executive committee and representatives from six apartments and six villas. Two types of groups are responsible to the council: first, ten function groups, which represent the gift shop, library, health center auxiliary, marketing volunteers, clubs and social groups, and special events; second, thirteen standing committees, which oversee activity groups, building and grounds, food service, welcoming, and sports.

Molly Crane, vice president of the council and a member of the finance and budget advisory committee, said the biggest issue recently before the association was a proposal to make the community smoke-free. Residents had strong feelings on this subject, so a secret vote was held, and by a three-to-one margin the residents voted not to legislate behavior. Eventually only the dining room, lounge, and meeting rooms were declared smoke-free.

Cooperation between the management and the residents is very good. "People are happy and get along well," Molly said. "Each person does his or her own thing. Most are into many activities, while others are not involved. This does not mean they are dissatisfied—it's just that they prefer more quiet time." Molly was a great help to us and we felt very positive about CM.

Carolina Meadows, P.O. Box 3484, Chapel Hill, NC 27514
800/458-6756

CAROL WOODS, CHAPEL HILL, NORTH CAROLINA

Openness and Participation in a Friendly Village

The following excerpts from the Carol Woods Disclosure Statement (May 30, 1993), which is given to all prospective residents, highlight the basic tenets of this community and the honest approach of the trustees and management.

Principles of Cooperation: The board expects management to work very closely with the residents through the association, its council and its committees. Each of the department managers meets routinely with the appropriate resident committees. This close working relationship was formalized in 1982. It is also used in budget preparation and rate setting.

Full Disclosure Practice: The annual audited financial statements and monthly unaudited financial statements are made available to the resident finance committee members and copies are placed in the library for residents

At Carol Woods, residents who choose garden apartments can participate in community activities while living independently.
(PHOTO COURTESY OF CAROL WOODS RETIREMENT CENTER IN CHAPEL HILL)

to read. Detailed budget briefings are given for all residents after budget approval.

Mission Statement: Commitment to a policy of maintaining in residence any persons who become unable to pay their regular charges due to circumstances beyond the control of the resident.

Couple the board's policy statements with the residents' responsibility for all community activities (there is no staff activity director), and the degree of resident involvement in running the community is clear.

After our arrival at Carol Woods we were ushered into a conference room set up for a slide presentation and discussion. We met:

Wesley H. Wallace, a resident since 1979, former

FINANCIAL INFORMATION—EXAMPLES, FOUR UNITS

TYPE	LIFE OCCUPANCY FEE		MONTHLY SERVICE FEE	
	Single	Double	Single	Double
Garden Apartments—1 Meal Daily				
1 bedroom, 678 sq. ft.	$ 70,000	$ 75,400	$1,506	$2,028
2 bedrooms/den, 1,343 sq. ft.	136,500	143,100	2,276	2,822
Central Apartments—3 Meals Daily				
Studio, 447 sq. ft.	41,800	N/A	1,482	N/A
2 bedrooms, 850 sq. ft.	94,800	97,400	2,013	2,718

chairman of the board of directors, and now a voting member. (Named to the Broadcasting Hall of Fame, he is a professor emeritus of radio, television and motion pictures and former department chairman at the University of North Carolina at Chapel Hill); Janet E. Campbell, president of the residents association, (former faculty member at the University of North Carolina at Chapel Hill); Patricia E. Sprigg, executive director; Rosemary A. Hutchinson, director of marketing/public relations.

Following a slide presentation we had an interesting in-depth discussion of the not-for-profit, 370-resident life-care community located on 120 acres.

Residents must be at least sixty-five at admission; a spouse may be no younger than fifty-five. A resident terminating the agreement at any time for any reason will receive a portion of the entry fee based on the number of months in residence, up to a maximum of fifty months. Each resident receives fifteen days inpatient care per year at the health center. Unused days accumulate from year to year. When all days are used, a discounted health care rate is charged.

Among the amenities, there are rooms for photography, woodworking, sewing, weaving, painting, ceramics, exercise, Ping-Pong, cards and games, a library, a lounge, and a large all-purpose meeting room. A bank, beauty/barber shop, gift shop, guest house, greenhouse, and new indoor pool also are on-site.

The residents association schedules and coordinates special events and continuing activities such as classical concerts, a Thursday night lecture series, book clubs, language clubs, investment clubs, discussion groups, dances, parties, and travel to area events.

Residents volunteer within the community. Some staff the information desk during the evening and weekends. Others participate in the chore brigade, hanging pictures and doing other odd maintenance jobs, which helps to keep expenses down. Members of the Ambassador's Club take prospective residents on tours or host them for lunch or dinner. A resident who had worked as a police chief assisted in updating community security, and a carpeting group did research toward carpet installation throughout the community.

Janet Campbell, president of the residents association, met with us and stressed the openness between management and residents. She said lengthy discussions are com-

CLIMATE—1991 TEMP. (°F), PRECIP. (IN.)				OF INTEREST—
	AVG.	MAX.	MIN.	PRECIP.	Winter weather usually includes some snow or sleet.
JAN.	41.9	66	19	4.12
APR.	62.3	86	36	1.04
JULY	80.6	96	67	10.27
OCT.	61.1	84	35	1.40

mon; residents express their views and then an amicable agreement is reached. Openness, free expression, and cooperation go hand in hand.

There was much activity as we toured the community, and we observed many thoughtful customs, such as a basket near the mailboxes where gardeners put their excess vegetables for residents to help themselves. A death is announced by placing a rose in a small vase next to an announcement card.

Carol Woods is AAHA Continuing Care Accredited.

Carol Woods, 750 Weaver Dairy Rd., Chapel Hill, NC 27514
919/968-4511

CASA DE LAS CAMPANAS, RANCHO BERNARDO, CALIFORNIA

A Place for Those Still Planning Ahead

We were on our way to an afternoon meeting of the Casa de las Campanas residents association when we were sur-

All apartments at Casa de las Campanas have a patio or balcony.
(PHOTO BY HENRY MEYER)

rounded by a large group of enthusiastic people chatting about the meeting. Each person carried a notebook or file as they left the three hundred-seat dinner theater. The meeting had adjourned before we were able to join them.

Kay Keith, director of residential sales, asked residents Fred and Betsy Schrupp if they would join us for a discussion about Casa. They accepted. We found a nearby lounge area and went through introductions and the purpose of our visit. The conversation soon took on an atmosphere of informality and congeniality.

Fred and his first wife were nineteenth on the list to move into Casa in August 1988. Before retirement he was a high school teacher, then a professor and later dean of the School of Education at San Diego State University.

In December 1989 his wife died of Alzheimer's disease. He spoke in glowing terms of the care given his wife in the health center. Fred later married Betsy, a nurse who cared for his wife in the medical center. Fred represents the recreation committee at association meetings. Both he and Betsy said that this is a very active, friendly community, and they feel good about how the management operates the complex.

Casa is a 426-apartment life-care community with a minimum age of sixty-two and is located within the master planned community of Rancho Bernardo, north of San Diego proper. It is an imposing complex of four connected buildings, each with four stories, made of stucco with red tile roofs. This hilltop community overlooks Lake Hodges and is adjacent to a 170-acre community park. I-15 is nearby.

The Foundation to Assist California Teachers (FACT), a non-profit organization with sixty years of experience in operating retirement and health care facilities, founded and manages Casa.

The community is minutes from North County Fair, San Diego's largest regional shopping mall. Nearby downtown Rancho Bernardo has four shopping centers, a movie theater, post office, library, and bank. A hospital is four minutes away, and San Diego International Airport (Lindbergh Field) is twenty-seven miles.

Casa was built with an initial investment of $80 million. Hallways, meeting rooms, lounges, dining rooms, and apartments are spacious, with no feeling of being crowded into cramped quarters. The average age is seventy-six, and 60 percent of the residents are couples. Occupancy is 85 percent. There is a waiting list for the larger apartments.

Amenities include two heated pools, outdoor exercise course and exercise center, two dining rooms, dinner theater, cocktail lounge, two laundry areas, arts/crafts and wood shop rooms, two libraries, game room, beauty/barber shop, two mail rooms, coffee shop, gift shop, and a ninety-nine-bed Medicare-approved skilled nursing facility with an adjacent assisted-living area.

Casa has four long buildings with apartments fronting on each side of the length of the building. Parking is in reserved spaces nearby. The buildings are connected by enclosed passageways. The health center adjoins the building near the entrance to the community. The complex completely fills the twenty-three acres.

Many factors influence the cost of a unit, including size, building and floor chosen, standard view, vista view, lake view, and one- or two-person occupancy. All units have a patio or balcony. Following are four examples of entrance and monthly service fees:

	ENTRANCE FEE	MONTHLY SERVICE FEE
Alcove, 547 sq. ft.	$ 72,300	$1,045
One bedroom, 784 sq. ft., Lake view, garden, or 3rd floor	115,000	1,300

	ENTRANCE FEE	MONTHLY SERVICE FEE
Two bedrooms, 1,135 sq. ft., Vista view	$151,500	$1,620
Unit L (large, deluxe unit), 1,921 sq. ft.	330,000	3,150
Second person	5,500	575

An optional refundable fee plan refunds up to 94 percent of the entrance fee if a resident cancels the residence agreement for any reason at any time; if the resident dies, the refund goes to his or her estate. Casa grants special financial assistance in most cases of unanticipated hardship.

A flexible meal system allows three meal values a day (breakfast is 1, lunch is 2, dinner is 3); residents may use these values any way they wish. Tray service is provided if necessary for medical reasons. Special diets ordered by the primary physician may be accommodated. Weekly linen service includes laundering of sheets, pillow cases, towels, and washcloths. Scheduled transportation service is provided by a van and two buses. All utilities except telephone and cable TV are included in residents' fees. Standard cleaning of each living unit is done every other week. Personal services can be arranged for occasional health problems; the assisted-living wing has a twenty-four-hour professional staff. The entrance fee and monthly service fee provide for twenty-four-hour nursing care in the health center. Limited garage parking is available for an additional fee. Also included is the use of all

CLIMATE—1991 TEMP. (°F), PRECIP. (IN.)				OF INTEREST—
	AVG.	MAX.	MIN.	PRECIP.
JAN.	57.4	79	42	1.06
APR.	61.7	80	51	0.05
JULY	67.4	76	60	0.24
OCT.	68.0	92	48	0.69

OF INTEREST— 85 percent of the annual rainfall occurs between November and March. Total precipitation in 1991 was 13.51 inches.

common and activity areas, emergency call system, security of building and grounds, fire detection system, and sprinkler systems.

A new sixteen-page brochure describing the community was just off the press when we surveyed. It was a well-written portrayal of Casa life—by a resident!

An important section of the brochure entitled "Responsive Management" reported that "the interactive climate constantly reflects the close rapport between the residents and management staff at all levels. . . . Resident input is encouraged for all budgets, plans and operations. . . . There is a fast reaction time to resident suggestions. . . . More than 30 active committees report on ongoing activities and ideas to the elected resident council. . . . Because the best resident is an informed resident, the channels of communication at Casa keep everyone aware of what's going on. . . . Whether it's new plantings, alterations to a building entry, a change in bus schedule, or the retrofitting of some lighting or air conditioning, you know when and why it's happening."

The symbol of Casa de las Campanas, whose name means "house of bells" in Spanish, is the carillon tower. The feeling of a campus is accentuated when the bells ring out significant hours of the day and help commemorate holidays.

Casa de las Campanas, 18655 West Bernardo Dr., San Diego, CA 92127
619/592-1870   800/554-6403

FREEDOM VILLAGE, HOLLAND, MICHIGAN

Home of Tulip Time in Holland Festival

Our interest in this life-care community was piqued when we had a lengthy discussion with our longtime friends Phyllis and Earl Sorenson.

During the early stages of construction the Sorensons

Freedom Village's main atrium includes a spiral staircase and grand piano.
(PHOTO COURTESY OF FREEDOM VILLAGE, HOLLAND)

began to consider moving to the village, which was scheduled to open in August 1991. They had been given a seventy-five-page disclosure document that covered all of the details. Included was a trust agreement guaranteeing that all residents would receive care for the rest of their life regardless of their physical or financial circumstances. All of the information sounded good, and we endorsed their decision to "join up." They made the move in early 1992.

Freedom Group, Inc., headquartered in Bradenton, Florida, manages the community. (The company operates fourteen similar communities in Arizona, California, and Florida.) This community, situated on a thirteen-acre plot in downtown Holland overlooking the Macatawa River, is a 348-unit, seven-story building with five wings, each named after one of the Great Lakes. It is red brick with white accents such as screened-in porches. The three-story entrance portico and two top floors are white stucco. There are eight apartment styles. Nearby is the long-term care facility, the Inn at Freedom Village.

APARTMENT STYLES	ENTRANCE FEE	MONTHLY FEE
Studio, 510 sq. ft.	$ 35,000–50,000	$ 791–818
Deluxe 1 bedroom/1 bath, 1,041 sq. ft.	91,000–120,000	1,055–1,240
Deluxe 2 bedrooms/2 baths, 1,344 sq. ft.	121,000–160,000	1,187–1,345
Second Person	5,000	422

As outlined in the Life Care Residency and Care Agreement, "Should you leave your residence at Freedom Village, for any reason, at least 50 percent of your entrance fee will be returned to you or your estate." Residents pay full price for only the first 120 days of care that deviates from independent living. After that they pay a reduced monthly fee for short-term care, assisted living, or skilled nursing—whatever level of care they need—for the rest of their life.

Services include the main meal of the day, utilities (except telephone), weekly housekeeping, linen service, cable TV, apartment maintenance, emergency call system, valet parking, uncovered parking space (carport or garage cost extra), local transportation, emergency medical care, around-the-clock security, and a health dynamics program.

The first floor contains the reception desk, a grand lobby (with atrium to the third floor), bank, post office, indoor swimming pool and spa, and outdoor patio. On the second floor is a deli, convenience store, game and card room, beauty parlor/barber shop, arts and crafts room, and woodworking shop. The third floor houses a medical clinic, library, billiard room, and meditation chapel. The fourth floor, which has a two-story ceiling, has an indoor padded walking track (sixteen times around equals one mile), exercise equipment, shuffleboard courts, and other indoor games. The sixth floor houses five dining rooms, each with its own distinctive decor, along with a private dining room and large auditorium/theater.

During our courting years in Grand Rapids, Michigan,

we traveled quite regularly the thirty miles to Holland beaches along Lake Michigan. We used to joke about their rolling up the sidewalks at 9:00 P.M. Now, in our maturing years, we feel this college town of 31,000 residents is wonderfully quiet, safe, and conservative.

The city of Holland, known for its annual May Tulip Festival, recently installed a "snow melt" system in the core of the downtown. The project buried fifty-eight miles of "loop" piping under 175,000 square feet of roads and brick sidewalks; when the pipes are filled with warm water, they prevent snow and ice accumulation. The "streetscope" project, currently in progress, includes the addition of one hundred historic lights, hundreds of trees, benches, and litter containers.

The downtown area is within three blocks of Freedom Village. Hope College, a coed liberal arts school founded in 1866 by the Reformed Church in America, has 2,800 students and abuts the south boundary of the village. Nearby highways are U.S. 31, M-21, M-40, and I-196. Also nearby is a 225-bed hospital, 25 parks, 74 churches representing 23 denominations, and 220 industries.

About a mile from the village is Evergreen Commons Senior Center. Of the many senior centers we've toured throughout the country, this 44,000-square-foot building is by far the best. It has a Senior Advocacy Center, Senior Day Care Center, a kitchen with a capacity for serving five hundred meals, and a Great Hall that can seat eight hundred people. It is another expression of the civic pride that is evident everywhere in Holland.

When we visited the Sorensons we were impressed

with the design, decorations, high-quality furnishings, and "first class" operations at the complex. Dinner in the Dutch Hearth dining room overlooking the river and Windmill Island, a municipal park with a two hundred-year-old, twelve-story working Dutch windmill, was outstanding.

Also worthy of note is the balcony on the second floor circling the Grand Lobby Atrium. Wood banisters and beveled glass panes in the room off the balcony add a touch of elegance to the circular stairway down to the first floor. Many residents like to play the grand piano in the first-floor lounge area.

Our friends have a 1,443-square-foot corner suite with two bedrooms and baths, a den, and two patios. It is very roomy, well decorated, and makes a great home. One built-in convenience we especially liked was a triangular receptacle by the front door for the morning paper, so residents don't have to stoop to pick it up—a great help to those with arthritis and back problems.

We maintain contact with Phyllis and Earl, and they continue to be happy with their decision to move to Freedom Village.

As noted in the climate statistics on the following page, this is cold winter country. This doesn't seem to hold back interest in the community, however, since it is 93 percent occupied with residents from eighteen states, Canada, and Japan. The monthly activity schedule provides a multitude of interesting opportunities, from an array of clubs to lectures and concerts. According to residents, there's no reason to have the winter doldrums.

CLIMATE—1991 TEMP. (°F), PRECIP. (IN.)				OF INTEREST—
	AVG.	MAX.	MIN.	PRECIP.
JAN.	24.5	42	6	1.36
APR.	49.1	77	19	3.56
JULY	71.1	90	49	3.31
OCT.	52.1	74	26	7.33

OF INTEREST—
Total snowfall was 68.6 inches in 1990–91, 136.8 inches in 1989–90. On average, the first 32°F day is October 11, and the last one May 8.

A well-designed retirement community in a small college town, Freedom Village is only thirty miles from Grand Rapids with its many hospitals and international airport—an environment for a great retirement.

Freedom Village, 145 Columbia Ave., Holland, MI 48423 800/622–5475

KIMBALL FARMS, LENOX, MASSACHUSETTS

New England Small Town Charm

"One of our residents came back from visiting relatives and said, 'They made me feel so old.' I agree with her," said Kimball Farms resident Peggy Halberstadt, a retired librarian who was putting the large community library in order when we stopped by to chat. She went on to say that the same thing happened to her on a recent trip. "Everyone was always asking if I was comfortable and taking my arm to help me along. Around here you are on your own—no one coddles you."

Kimball Farms is surrounded by lush Berkshire woods.
(PHOTO BY CLEMENS KALISCHER)

We surveyed Kimball Farms on a Saturday morning when most residents were at the nearby Tanglewood Music Festival. Itzhak Perlman was the featured performer. Many residents like to attend the Saturday open rehearsals, and some stay on for the evening performance.

Kimball Farms is an attractive life-care community nestled in the Berkshire Hills. We found many innovative features that offer opportunities for informal interaction. For example, an open potting shed with skylights was built off one of the main areas as a place for people to gather and chat with the gardeners. The Country Store has been designed to encourage chitchat over midmorning coffee as the residents drop in for sundry items. To bring the entire community together, "Friendly Friday" takes place once a week in the Gathering Room of the Commons during the cocktail hour.

The 150-unit, 190-resident community opened in November 1989. It is located on sixty-three acres of heavily wooded terrain in western Massachusetts, ten miles from the New York state line, seven miles north of I-90 and ten miles south of Pittsfield. The nearest airport is in Albany, New York, fifty miles to the west.

This community has a 90-percent-refundable entry fee. There are seven apartment floor plans. Cost of the largest two-bedroom apartment is:

Entrance Fee	Single Occupancy	Double Occupancy
	$202,400	$209,900
Monthly Fee	Single Occupancy	Double Occupancy
	$2,868	$3,394

Amenities and services include a library and reading room; fitness center; beauty salon/barber shop; banking and postal services; country store and gift shop; laundry facilities on each floor; central auditorium for meetings, guest speakers, religious services, and cultural events; garden plots; a parlor with fireplace and abundant conversation areas; one meal a day; regular local transportation; all utilities except telephone; security system; and health supervision and use of the forty-one-bed Medicare-approved nursing care center for short-term recuperative stays or longer-term nursing care.

Charter resident Newcombe Cole invited us to his

apartment. A member of the preconstruction ad hoc committee who has held offices and committee appointments in the residents association, he is a delightful, pipe-smoking country gentleman, legally blind and extremely proud of Kimball Farms. He feels secure and content knowing that whatever assistance he needs, or might need, is always near at hand.

In the late eighties, during one of our research trips, we journeyed to the town of Lenox, renowned as a gathering place for the nation's early millionaires. We were captivated by its New England charm.

In the center of town is the former Curtis Hotel, which features a wraparound porch, located next door to the old Berkshire County Courthouse, a structure built in 1815 that now serves as the library. Miscellaneous small shops line the streets. Some of the sandstone sidewalks were uneven, caused by roots of the giant shade trees.

A short distance away we located the site of Kimball Farms, occupied at the time by an immense red barn and a large, battered old farmhouse. We determined that we would someday return to see the finished product.

CLIMATE—1991 TEMP. (°F), PRECIP. (IN.)				OF INTEREST—
	AVG.	MAX.	MIN.	PRECIP.
JAN.	23.2	44	−4	2.15
APR.	51.2	87	25	4.14
JULY	71.6	97	47	1.65
OCT.	53.2	78	28	3.82

OF INTEREST— Lenox is in the Berkshire Hills. Summer temperatures tend to be more moderate and winters more severe than recorded at the Albany, New York, weather station.

A group of private citizens and medical professionals dreamed of building a superior community to meet the needs of people sixty-five years of age and older. We returned in August 1993 and found that the dream had been fulfilled in every respect.

Kimball Farms, 193 Walker St., Lenox, MA 01240
413/637-4684   800/283-0061

RAPPAHANNOCK WESTMINSTER-CANTERBURY, IRVINGTON, VIRGINIA

Chesapeake Bay Charm

A Palm Sunday lunch with four "Sprysters" introduced us to this community located in the "Northern Neck," which in other parts of the country would be known as a peninsula. Here it's the northernmost neck of Virginia's shoreline where the Potomac and Rappahannock rivers empty into Chesapeake Bay. It is made up of five counties with about 58,000 people. Captain John Smith and the Indian princess Pocahontas walked these lands about four hundred years ago.

The quaint old town of Irvington is in the southwest corner of the Neck, a few miles from the bridge to the "mainland." Kilmarnock is a short distance north and is much larger than Irvington.

RW-C opened in 1985 and is located on 113 acres of woodlands and meadows. Connected by covered walk-

Rappahannock Westminster-Canterbury features forty apartments, seventy-eight cottages, and a sixty-bed health center.

ways to the Chesapeake Center are forty apartments, seventy-eight cottages, and a sixty-bed health center. All structures are made of wood and have a gray, weathered look that blends into this tidelands area. Roads are laid out to allow for future expansion. This is a not-for-profit life-care community guided by the high standards and Christian values set down by the Episcopal and Presbyterian churches to which it is related. It is through these two churches that the trustees of RW-C are elected.

FOUNDER'S AND MONTHLY FEES

Example—2 bedroom/2 bath apartment, 1,120 sq. ft.; cottage 1,103 sq. ft.:

	FOUNDER'S FEE		MONTHLY FEE	
	One Person	Second Person	One Person	Second Person
Apartment	$145,355	$39,750	$1,938	$680
Cottage	153,870	39,750	2,078	680

REFUND OPTIONS IN BRIEF

There are three refund options. Under all three, the monthly fee does not increase when the resident moves from independent living to a higher level of care. Options one and two allow for twenty-five-month and fifty-month refunds, respectively, with deductions for each month of residence. Option three offers a guaranteed minimum refund of 50 percent regardless of when death or withdrawal occurs. Prospective residents should make a detailed analysis of *all* conditions of each option to see which suits them best.

Services and amenities include one meal daily; weekly housekeeping; all utilities except telephone; maintenance of residence, common areas, buildings, and grounds; local transportation; community security; cable TV; emergency call system; social, recreational, and educational activities; dietetic consultant for special diets; clinic and wellness-fitness program; laundry facilities; library; private dining room for special occasions; craft room, arts program, and woodworking shop; garden plots; exercise trail, woodland paths, and biking roads; enclosed heated swimming pool; beauty/barber shop; café/deli; convenience store; and banking. The entire grounds are barrier-free.

"Northern Neck" cultural activities, sponsored by various organizations, include Lancaster County Garden Tours; a concert series sponsored by the Rappahannock Foundation for the Arts; books and coffee at the County Library; and productions by the Lancaster Players. At RW-C the Rappahannock Chamber Choir gave a concert, and the Swift Creek Mill Playhouse presented "Cotton Patch Gospel."

There is a clinic on-site, and the nearest hospital is in Kilmarnock, five miles away. Richmond hospitals are sixty-two miles away.

We asked our Palm Sunday lunch group, "Do many people leave?" "Maybe four or five," they said, but usually as a result of personal taste. One lady's reason for going back to New Mexico, for example, was "It's too green here"—she missed the brown earth. The people we met had been at RW-C at least six years and were enthusiastic about their extended family of "wonderful, stimulating" residents at the community. It was a terrific Palm Sunday for us. We felt we made some new friends.

The mission of the RW-C Foundation is to provide support for RW-C, Inc., by encouraging and supporting the community's volunteer program and by raising funds for fellowship assistance and other RW-C ventures. We were told that nine residents with financial problems were receiving assistance. This is truly life care for those who have encountered financial setbacks.

The foundation's 1992 annual report featured a picture of Elizabeth Gray, RW-C Foundation trustee and RW-C resident, as she took her first balloon ride over the

CLIMATE—1991 TEMP. (°F), PRECIP. (IN.)				OF INTEREST—
	AVG.	MAX.	MIN.	PRECIP.
JAN.	43.5	72	19	4.74
APR.	61.6	88	35	6.39
JULY	82.0	100	66	6.46
OCT.	61.9	86	42	4.65

OF INTEREST— Total precipitation in 1991 was 42.92 inches. On average, the first 32°F day is November 17, the last one March 23. Only a trace of snow fell in 1990–91.

nearby countryside on her eightieth birthday. She said this topped the elephant ride on her seventy-fifth! We came away with the feeling that she represented RW-C, accepting aging and living life to the fullest.

Rappahannock Westminster-Canterbury, 10 Lancaster Dr., Irvington, VA 22480
804/438-4000

THE MOORINGS, ARLINGTON HEIGHTS, ILLINOIS

A 45-Acre Oasis in the City

Our introduction to this community started at an Elder-hostel program in Mesa, Arizona, in February 1989. Two of our classmates were Bill and Jean Cremens of Chicago. They moved to The Moorings in July of 1990 after thirty years in the same house—quite a change!

We wrote them about our first book and they sent a glowing letter about life at The Moorings. An analysis of the material we received prompted us to survey the facility.

The hub of activity at The Moorings of Arlington Heights is the Midrise Building.

Bill and Jean informed The Moorings administration of our desire to survey the community, and we were invited to spend the night in the community guest accommodations. We gratefully accepted. We met many of the residents and learned a great deal about this style of living.

The Moorings is owned and operated by Lutheran General Senior Services and is located twenty-three miles northwest of the Chicago Loop. The train station is three miles from the community, and it is a forty-five minute ride to downtown Chicago.

This is a life-care retirement community for adults sixty-two years of age and older. It includes 291 apartments and single-story two-bedroom villas located on forty-five acres. The central complex is five stories high with two four-story wings. A one hundred-bed health center is connected to the main building. Around the perimeter are thirty villa buildings. Two large lakes encircle three sides of the main building, and walking paths provide adequate exercise routes. All buildings are made of red brick.

The Moorings is surrounded by an upper middle class, single-family residential neighborhood. The entrance is off Central Road, a six-lane divided street with shops, churches, and restaurants nearby. Arlington Heights has a population of over 75,000, making the Moorings complex truly an oasis in the city.

The Moorings has one entrance and the security gate is manned twenty-four hours a day. Originally this was farmland, and the unique one hundred-year-old round barn still stands. Buildings, roads, and grounds are well planned and immaculate.

Residents can choose from five apartment and two villa styles. The chart on the following page lists costs of two apartments and one villa with bath, Founder's and Endowment Fees.

Apartments include electric range and frost-free refrigerator, individually controlled heating and air conditioning, wall-to-wall carpeting and mini-blinds, an emergency response system, and a separate small storage area.

Villas include above apartment features and attached garage, patio, washer and dryer, fireplace, dishwasher and disposal.

Services and amenities include continental breakfast and one additional meal daily, weekly housekeeping, flat linen service, regularly scheduled transportation, basic

F = Founder's Fee/E = Endowment Fee			Monthly Fee/ Same for (F) or (E)	
Residence		1 Person	2 Persons	1 Person	2 Persons

Residence		1 Person	2 Persons	1 Person	2 Persons
1-bedroom, patio/Balcony	(F)	$ 72,000	$ 82,000	$1,239	$1,937
	(E)	112,900	122,900	1,239	1,937
2-bedroom, Corner	(F)	97,000	107,000	1,419	2,117
	(E)	167,375	177,375	1,419	2,117
2-bedroom End Villa	(F)	142,500	182,500	1,548	2,246
	(E)	245,300	255,300	1,548	2,246

(F) *Founder's Fee*—Not refundable after twenty-four months of residency; reduced 4 percent a month for the first twenty-four months.

(E) *Endowment Fee*—Reduced 4 percent at the time of a unit deposit and 1 percent per month for the first sixteen months of occupancy, after which an 80 percent refund will be paid to the resident or resident's estate if the unit is vacated.

cable TV, laundry facilities, all utilities except telephone, outside parking (heated underground parking available at additional cost), access to health services (such as outpatient services and health education programs), meditation room, indoor heated swimming pool, game and card rooms, fitness center with whirlpool, woodworking shop, painting studio, arts and crafts room, billiards room, convenience store, beauty/barber shop, and private dining rooms.

Why did Bill and Jean move to The Moorings? During the Elderhostel program in Arizona, they had told us of their plan to move to a retirement community some-day. After Bill had a slight heart attack, they took action. The Moorings is one mile from each of their two daughters and three grandchildren. They did a great deal of investigating, put their house up for sale, and chose a two-bedroom, two-bath unit on the fifth floor, facing east. On those rare clear days they can see the Chicago skyline.

We discussed the question of living with a "bunch of old people." They agreed that it's a somewhat cloistered type of living, but a look in the mirror shows that they fit right in!

Residents like to tell a joke about a newcomer who asked if someone could point out Mary Smith and was told that Mary was the silver-haired lady in the white sweater. Then they laugh, because as you look around the dining room, it is filled with "little old silver-haired ladies" in white sweaters.

They explained that in a retirement community the realities of getting old are openly accepted and "we all live with it." Griping and complaining about health problems is not tolerated. Those who tend to be negative band together and are not in the mainstream of community life. The positive acceptance of reality builds the camaraderie of an extended family.

We experienced this firsthand during our visit. The night we were there, one of the "silver-haired" widows was taken to the hospital. At breakfast the next morning there was a commotion at the entrance to the dining room. The woman had returned from the hospital and at least twenty people had gathered around her. There was

CLIMATE—1991 TEMP. (°F), PRECIP. (IN.)				OF INTEREST—
	AVG.	MAX.	MIN.	PRECIP.
JAN.	20.8	44	-3	1.41
APR.	52.0	83	26	4.00
JULY	75.5	101	53	1.32
OCT.	53.2	80	28	7.36

OF INTEREST—
Total precipitation in 1991 was 35.02 inches. On average, the first 32°F day is in mid-October, the last in late April. Snowfall in 1990–91 was 23.5 inches.

much hugging as she was welcomed home. A stream of people visited her table with a cheerful word. This was extended-family community in action.

The monthly activity calendar lists a full schedule. In fact, activities are listed on the front and health and fitness on the back. Activities offered during one month of 1993 included painting, pinochle, choir rehearsal, ceramics, Bible study, fabric painting, bingo, flower arranging, creative writing, sing-along, social hour, book group, movies, speakers, musical presentations, and cultural activities in town. Health/fitness activities included chair exercise, strength training, water aerobics, walking, stretching, and Richard Simmons videos. Most of these take place weekly.

Our experience at The Moorings was very satisfying. Those whom we talked to were in the prime of life—in a slower lane than in their younger years, but still going strong.

The Moorings, 811 E. Central Rd., Arlington Heights, IL 60005
708/437-6700

Residents of The Renaissance can live in apartments (right) or in single-story townhouses that comprise four neighborhoods.

THE RENAISSANCE, OLMSTED TOWNSHIP, OHIO

Right in the Middle of a Golf Course

A 164-acre, eighteen-hole golf course was purchased by the Eliza Jennings Group and the middle 74 acres were used to build The Renaissance. In the center of the community is a three-story, 97-apartment independent-living complex and community building. In addition, there is assisted living and a 120-bed health center, including a 45-bed wing for people with Alzheimer's disease.

Around the perimeter of the central complex are five neighborhoods, each consisting of fourteen townhouses built around a cul-de-sac. The golf course (open to the public) circles the entire community. There are no greens fees for residents.

Amenities include the Renaissance dining room for nightly dining (thirty meals per month), the Bistro sidewalk café, private dining room, tap room, meeting rooms, game and club room, chapel, library, beauty/barber shop, gift and sundry shop, full-service banking, emergency response system, physical fitness center, individual mailboxes, stocked lake, greenhouse, garden plots, on- and off-site scheduled transportation, concierge service, weekly housekeeping, grounds maintenance, and programs of social, cultural, educational, and recreational activities.

The community is located in a residential area about twenty-five minutes south of downtown Cleveland. Shopping, medical services, hospitals, and Cleveland-Hopkins International Airport are readily accessible.

FINANCIAL ARRANGEMENTS

ENTRANCE FEE	ONE PERSON	TWO PERSONS
2-bedroom apartment	$126,700	$147,300
2-bedroom townhouse	158,000	176,000

After occupancy, refunds are based on a deduction of 1 percent per month during the first five years. After the fifth year there will always be a refund of 40 percent of the entrance fee if the resident moves permanently to the medical center, leaves, or dies. This fee covers life use of the residence, life use of the health clinic, and up to fourteen days of care per year per person in the health center (for recuperation from temporary illness or convalescence from hospital stay).

NOTE: When leaving an apartment or townhouse for permanent residency in the medical center, the resident receives the entrance fee refund, which can then be applied to the cost of nursing care.

MONTHLY FEE	ONE PERSON	SECOND PERSON
2-bedroom apartment	$1,690	$595 additional
2-bedroom townhouse	1,810	595 additional

We were invited to the townhouse of Bob and Mary Dixon, who are charter members of the community. Bob, a retired trial lawyer for the U.S. government, is chairman of the residents association. He told us that there is very good communication and sharing of all information, especially financial condition, between the association and the community administration. For example, the residents association gets the same quarterly financial report that is given to each board member. Both of the Dixons were very content with their lifestyle.

Mary said that the reputation of the Eliza Jennings Home was highly influential in their choosing The Renaissance. This home in Cleveland was founded in 1887 as a women's residence. Today the home administers its services under the umbrella of the Eliza Jennings Group, including The Renaissance and E. J. Services, Inc., which

CLIMATE—1991 TEMP. (°F), PRECIP. (IN.)				
	AVG.	MAX.	MIN.	PRECIP.
JAN.	27.3	52	-1	2.18
APR.	52.6	82	22	4.22
JULY	74.7	97	54	1.69
OCT.	55.7	81	31	2.65

OF INTEREST—
Total precipitation in 1991 was 32.67 inches. Winters have an average of five days with subzero temperatures. On average, the first 32°F day occurs in October, the last in April. Snowfall in 1990–91 was 47.1 inches.

provides broad management services to various types of retirement living communities throughout the country. We also spoke with a member of the board of trustees. We asked her what would happen if a Renaissance resident ran out of funds while residing in the medical center. She replied, "We have never put anyone out in 105 years."

The Renaissance, named after the magnificent historical period of intellectual vigor and personal growth, today exemplifies high standards and security in a troubled world.

The Renaissance, 26376 John Rd., Olmsted Twp., OH 44138
216/235-7111

FUTURE

Glenaire, Cary, North Carolina

We said hello to Dr. Samuel M. Stone, a Presbyterian minister, licensed nursing home administrator, fundraiser, and "pressured" executive director of Glenaire. Very early in our conversation we learned that although the project was three months behind schedule, it was 87 percent reserved, and people were moving in daily. Our conversation was interrupted by one of the dozens of messages he deals with throughout the day: "Mrs. X" wanted her towel rack put up immediately.

We told him we understood the demands on his time and asked if we could wander around. "By all means," he replied, "if you can find your way into the buildings." Someday we want to go back and finish our conversation; he seemed to be a fine gentleman.

This continuing-care community is located on thirty wooded acres in a pleasant residential area, close to everything. The town of Cary is a bedroom suburb of Raleigh and has a population of about 50,000. Anyone sixty-five or older may be admitted to the community, with a spouse of at least sixty-two. Two three-story apartment buildings connect to one end of the community building, and the health center adjoins the opposite side of the building. Duplex cottages are clustered around a small pond.

We could not get into the main building because of construction vehicles; there were workers all over the complex. Overlooking what appeared to be organized confusion, however, we felt that in the future this will become a top-notch continuing care community. It is a division of Presbyterian Homes, Inc., and is affiliated with the Presbyterian Church (USA) through the Synod of the Mid-Atlantic.

Glenaire, P.O. Box 4322, Cary, NC 27519
919/460-8095

Sandhill Cove, Stuart, Florida

Thirty-six acres situated on Pendarvis Cove at the St. Lucie River's south fork is the site of this life-care community. Opened in August 1993, it has the advantage of close proximity to the village of Martin Downs, a master planned community with an abundance of activities and conveniences.

The developer/management company is a subsidiary of Life Care Services Corporation of Des Moines, Iowa. This corporation has planned, developed, or managed over sixty retirement communities throughout the United States for more than three decades. As of February 1992 it had four communities in the development stage.

In total Sandhill Cove will have 168 one-, two-, and two-bedroom-with-den apartments and villas. The apartments are in two separate two-story buildings: The Gardens in the center of the complex, and The Waterside overlooking the river. Both connect with Sandhill Club, the activity center. A thirty-bed health center also connects to the club. Fourteen two-unit villas are on the periphery of the community.

The following services are included in the monthly service fee: one meal each day in the formal dining room, which serves three meals a day; indoor/outdoor maintenance and housekeeping of apartments and common areas; weekly flat laundry service; real estate taxes; utilities, excluding telephone and electricity; residence emergency call system connected to the health center; regularly scheduled transportation; health care in the on-site health center; twenty-four-hour security; and planned social, cultural, and recreational activities.

Entrance fees begin at $161,000 and go as high as $371,000. A special "return of capital" plan allows for up to 90 percent of the entrance fee to be refunded to the resident or the resident's estate upon departure or death. Monthly service fees range from $1,430 to $2,260, plus $730 for a second person.

The location, architecture, and aura of spaciousness make this a desirable option for those considering an upscale life-care community.

Sandhill Cove, P.O. Box 3116, Stuart, FL 34995
407/220-1090

Westminster at Lake Ridge, Lake Ridge, Virginia

Going north on I-95, about twenty miles south of Washington, D.C., we exited on Route 123 and found our way to the small town of Lake Ridge, a bedroom community for the nation's capital. A wrong turn took us down a steep hill into several blocks of restored buildings that are now gift shops, boutiques, and restaurants. This old section of town stretched all the way down to a small dock in the backwaters of a dam in the Occoquan River. Eventually we gave up and asked for directions to Westminster. Up the hill and into the "real world" of fast-food restaurants and apartments, we found Clipper Drive. After we passed Lake Ridge Baptist Church and Rockledge Elementary School, a sixty-acre bowl-shaped clearing came into view, completely surrounded by heavy woods. Ground was broken for this non-profit community on January 30, 1992, and it opened in January 1993. It will have a total of 192 independent units, both apartments and cottages. In March 1993 a few connected cottages, four to a unit, were occupied, and many more were under construction. A large, impressive three-story red brick community center and apartment building on a knoll overlooking the entire community was a busy place, with workmen scurrying around and prospective residents touring the models.

This is a continuing-care facility and will require an entrance fee as well as a monthly fee. The health care center will include assisted living and intermediate and skilled nursing care. It is owned by Westminster Presbyterian Retirement Community Inc.

Westminster at Lake Ridge, 12531 Clipper Dr., #101, Lake Ridge, VA 22192
703/643-0551

SPECIAL INTEREST COMMUNITIES

MILITARY

Camaraderie, the foundation of the professional military experience, is also a central feature of the RCs for retired military officers. Not all residents in these RCs are retired military, but the vast majority have had military careers.

Each of the RCs that we surveyed in this category was the picture of military precision: neat, orderly, well maintained, and first class. High morale was the order of the day and came through loud and clear.

AIR FORCE VILLAGE II, SAN ANTONIO, TEXAS

Military Uniformity

We told the gatehouse officer, Joe Cunningham, that we had an appointment with Fred Muise director of admis-

Air Force Village II contains apartment towers, a health center, and round garden homes connected by carports.
(PHOTO COURTESY OF MARK LANGFORD PHOTOGRAPHY)

sions and marketing. An ear-to-ear smile took over as he said, "Welcome, we're glad that you're here." We gave him our names, and he showed sincere enthusiasm as he told us how he came over from Air Force Village I and "raised the flag" here. "This is the best place there is," he said.

We drove up the curving lane past the new garden homes, twelve to a cul-de-sac, two to a structure, separated by two garages. All had precisely the same architecture, roof, and brick red color.

The village center connects two V-shaped eight-story apartment towers. A one-story health care center adjoins one of the towers. Beyond the center are the original

garden homes built at the same time as the towers, in
1986–87. Each of these round buildings contains two
units separated by a carport, in the same color as the
towers. Interspersed on the grounds are three landscaped
lakes and an RV storage area.

Fred Jones, executive director of AFV II, explained
the functioning of the Air Force Village Foundation and
AFV II:

■ AFV I, five miles east with a similar layout,
opened in 1970. AFV II opened in 1987, and construction is near completion on an expansion of forty-four
garden homes, all sold.

■ Both villages operate under the umbrella of the
AFV Foundation and are tax-exempt organizations
under IRS Code 501(C)3.

■ These are life-care communities for retired Air
Force officers, widows in need, widows/widowers, de-
pendents, and active-duty spouses.

■ AFV II has 208 tower apartments, 152 garden
apartments, a 32-room (68 beds) health care center,
and covered parking for tower residents. Of the 350
female residents, 95 are single. Twenty-eight of the
280 male residents are single. There is a waiting list
for new residents. The average age in the apartments
is seventy-two; in the Health Care Center, eighty.

As we toured, the influence of military training was evident: a place for everything and everything in place. The

buildings have plenty of windows, comfortable furniture, and a high-ceiling dining room with a nice view. The health care center provides a private dining room for celebrations—anniversaries, birthdays, or other occasions—complete with flowers, candlelight dinner, and elegant service. The complex is built on 145 acres surrounded by open country, twenty miles west of downtown San Antonio on U.S. 90, five miles beyond the I-410 loop. The largest Air Force hospital, Wilford Hall, is located at Lackland Air Force Base, seven miles away; Kelly Air Force Base is eleven miles away. There are ten tower apartment designs. Costs for the smallest (one bedroom, one bath, 664 sq. ft.) include a nonrefundable founders fee of $59,760 and monthly fee of $704. Costs for the largest (two bedrooms, two baths, 1,312 sq. ft.): founders fee, non refundable, $118,080; monthly fee, $1,391. Garden apartment costs are comparable based on size. Each resident is billed $115 per month which is applied to the cost of individually priced meals ordered from the menu. Additional meal costs are billed separately. Monthly electric bills are sent to all apartments. A daily rate charged to each resident in the health care center is substantially lower than prevailing rates in other private nursing homes. Amenities include weekly housekeeping, emergency nursing care, library, music and recreation rooms, chapels, craft center, woodworking shop, beauty shop, fitness center, indoor pool, tennis courts, garden plots, and scheduled transportation.

At our meeting with five residents, all stressed that

the residents play a large role in community management through participation in:

■ Residents Representative Committee (liaison with management)
■ Activities Coordinating Committee (fifty resident activity groups)
■ Dining Room Advisory Committee (liaison with management)
■ High Flight Chapel Policy Committees (three faith groups)

In addition, two task forces have been formed to study the need for an Alzheimer's wing and to develop a strategic plan for the future. It's evident that high resident involvement translates into high morale.

Air Force Village II, 5100 John D. Ryan Blvd., San Antonio, TX 78245
210/677-8666   800/762-1122

CLIMATE—1991 TEMP. (°F), PRECIP. (IN.)				OF INTEREST—
	AVG.	MAX.	MIN.	PRECIP.
JAN.	48.9	81	30	5.08
APR.	72.4	90	42	4.91
JULY	84.5	103	71	2.23
OCT.	73.3	99	39	0.87

OF INTEREST— Total precipitation in 1991 was 42.76 inches. Summer temperatures exceed 90°F about 80 percent of the time. Temperatures fall below 32°F about 20 days per year. Snow is rare.

FLEET LANDING, ATLANTIC BEACH, FLORIDA

Home Port

Can retired navy skippers stay away from the water? Of course not! That's why Fleet Landing, a not-for-profit life-care facility, was built around a seven-acre lake. When wind conditions are favorable, a fleet of three dinghies, each with a skipper and "crew of one," competes for sailing honors. This well-designed community, about one-half mile from the Atlantic Ocean, is home to retired military officers and their spouses. The majority are retired from the navy.

Jacksonville, Florida, is the nation's largest city in land mass, with 840 square miles for more than 700,000 residents. It is located in northern Florida where the St. Johns River empties into the Atlantic Ocean. Seventy-two-acre Fleet Landing is in the Jacksonville/Atlantic Beach area, two miles from Mayport Naval Station. A new area commissary and Naval Exchange is located near the "back" entrance to Fleet Landing. The services and amenities of Cecil Field Naval Air Station are also available.

The governing body of this community is Naval Continuing Care Retirement Foundation, Inc. A board of directors administers the foundation's affairs. Opening day was December 1, 1990; it is 82 percent occupied, and 80 percent of the occupants are couples. The average age is seventy-three.

Although the community is primarily navy, retired officers of any of the military services are welcome. Others eligible are surviving spouses of retired U.S. military officers; U.S. Public Health and NOAA officers and spouses; surviving spouses of officers who died while on active duty or who are missing in action, and others determined by the board. All residents must be at least sixty-two years old.

There are three entrance fee refund plans—no refund, 50 percent, and 95 percent—which vary with the size of the living unit. There are twelve unit options. Following are examples of costs for a "middle size" apartment and house, as of May 1, 1993.

---

2 BEDROOM/2 BATH, DELUXE APT.	2 BEDROOM/2 BATH, DELUXE PATIO HOME
50% refund entrance fee— $159,753	50% refund entrance fee— $173,761
Monthly fee—$1,211	Monthly fee—$1,306

For a second person add entrance fee—$4,326; monthly fee—$482.

Services and amenities provided for the monthly fee include: credit for thirty meals per month (three meals a day are served); special diet meal preparation; all utilities except premium cable TV and telephone; weekly housekeeping service; flatwork linen laundry; maintenance in each residence and periodic redecorating; emergency call system; security patrol and gated entrance; scheduled transportation; banking and postal services; grounds maintenance; heated spa and swimming pool; use of tennis and shuffleboard courts and game rooms; convenience store; beauty/barber shop; hobby/woodworking shop; access to health club, including exercise and fitness classes; and scheduled social programs. Residents are guaranteed a skilled nursing or assisted living bed in the health center at a discounted rate when needed. Emergency nursing care anywhere on the Fleet Landing grounds and outpatient nursing services in the health center are covered as well.

It is a policy of the board to avoid asking any resident to leave because of an inability to pay, provided such inability is due to no fault of the resident and that such action does not jeopardize the financial stability of Fleet Landing.

Paula Disy, director of marketing, saw that our survey got off to a great start by introducing us to Executive Director Leo V. Rabuck, Captain, USN Retired. He said the community emphasizes the "care" part of life care. "Our residents make the 'care' happen," he said. "The motto established by the residents is 'Residents helping residents.' "

Our host at lunch was Art Lynn, president of the nine-member residents council. He attends all foundation board meetings as an ex officio member and said, "Relations with the administration are excellent." The council oversees a suggestion system: a copy of each resident suggestion is sent to the executive director, who replies directly to the writer. Art commented, "The suggestion system works extremely well."

CLIMATE—1991 TEMP. (°F), PRECIP. (IN.)				OF INTEREST—
	AVG.	MAX.	MIN.	PRECIP.
JAN.	56.3	83	30	10.20
APR.	72.3	94	44	6.31
JULY	83.8	98	70	15.90
OCT.	70.9	88	48	6.36

OF INTEREST— Total precipitation in 1991 was 79.63 inches, the most in 30 years. Average humidity is 75 percent. In summer, it rains one out of every two days.

Fleet Landing residents are active in civic affairs and volunteer work within and outside of the community. In the Jacksonville Senior Games residents brought home twenty gold, eight silver, and six bronze medals.

Our feelings about Fleet Landing echoed those of the residents: It's a terrific place!

Fleet Landing, One Fleet Landing Blvd., Atlantic Beach, FL 32233
904/246-9900   800/USA-USN1

THE FAIRFAX, FORT BELVOIR, VIRGINIA

The Objective Is Secured

Each December before the Army-Navy football game the cheerleaders and band from West Point journey to The Fairfax to participate in the traditional rally party. Residents of this life-care community, retired officers from all branches of the service, undoubtedly experience great pride as the colors are presented and the national anthem played. Tears may creep down cheeks of those who participated in previous games as they relive the past service rivalry, then are forgotten as the unity of Fairfax community life overshadows their memories.

Col. Bob Cook is chairman of the Fairfax residents council, the governing body of the residents association. He talked with us at length about the feeling of family that has evolved at the Fairfax since it opened on September 9, 1989. "We have no rules or regulations," he said. "All of these folks know how to live together." Another important point that he covered had to do with the continuance of comradeship—the dependence upon each other during combat or when assignments disrupt normal family living. This is just as important to retired officers as it was when they were on active duty.

As we talked in an alcove off the community center's main lobby, we observed a high level of camaraderie among the residents as they went about their business. The concierge's desk was the focal point for many conversations and friendly greetings. Judging from what we observed during our survey, we thought the average age would be in the late sixties—but in reality, it is seventy-six.

The Army Retirement Residence Foundation–Potomac (ARRF-P) was incorporated as a not-for-profit foundation in 1983. Its purpose was to develop retirement residences in the Washington, D.C., area for retired army officers with twenty years of active duty, and spouses or surviving spouses. In 1991 the membership was expanded to include retired officers from all branches of the armed services.

Through a subsidiary, the Marriott Corporation operates and owns all of the issued stock of The Fairfax under an intricate agreement with ARRF-P. The joint sponsorship is designed to ensure the continued operation of the community at high, but fiscally responsible, standards.

The community is located adjacent to Fort Belvoir at the intersection of Richmond Highway and Telegraph Road. The health care center is connected to the community building and has a separate entrance. Five mid-rise apartment buildings are connected by enclosed walkways to the community center. Thirty-five four-unit cottages are grouped around cul-de-sacs. Throughout the facility we saw the noticeable influence of Marriott's interior decorating service.

The center of the complex features parade grounds, and an imposing three-story clock tower adjoins the community building. Louis Varella, our Marriott host, told us that the clock must be exactly on time—military precision prevails.

The first floor of the community building houses the main dining room and two smaller dining areas, along with a kitchen, mail room, library, gift shop, country store/coffee shop, bank, beauty shop, barber shop, chapel, meeting room, dining room auditorium, four lobby lounge areas, and three terraces that overlook the manicured grounds. In the lower level are the administration offices; a health club with locker rooms, heated pool and whirlpool; rooms for exercise, arts and crafts, woodworking, and cards; and a computer learning center. Outdoors are walking trails, a putting green, gazebo, and picnic area.

Residents have access to the Fort Belvoir officers' club, commissary, DeWitt Army Medical Center, and the post recreational facilities including golf, swimming, tennis, hobby and craft shop, gymnasium, and marina. There is regularly scheduled bus service between the community and Fort Belvoir. Three other major hospitals are available in the nearby Washington, D.C., area.

There are 382 independent-living residences, plus a health center with 45 assisted-living units and a 60-bed nursing care center. There are two fee plans; each refunds 95 percent of the entry fee. One plan has a high entry fee and low monthly fee, the other has a low entry fee and high monthly fee. Apartments vary in size from 602 to 1,500 square feet; cottages range from 1,140 to 1,527 square feet. Examples of cost variance for two sizes of apartments are on the following page.

Fees include one meal a day, weekly housekeeping, emergency call system, security personnel on duty twenty-four hours, parking for one car (covered parking is extra), maintenance of all community-owned items in the apartment, grounds maintenance, utilities (except telephone), scheduled transportation, and planned events and activities.

The long-term care cost-protection program is included in the monthly fee. When combined with Medicare and a supplemental plan, in most cases, the majority

ORIGINAL PLAN	ENTRANCE FEE	MONTHLY FEE
1 bedroom	$100,500– 174,400	$1,294–1,357
2 bedrooms	154,600– 252,700	1,488–1,682
MODERATE PLAN	ENTRANCE FEE	MONTHLY FEE
1 bedroom	$ 50,250– 87,200–	$1,665–1,798
2 bedrooms	77,300– 126,350–	2,046–2,430

Add $6,500 (nonrefundable) life-care fee and $566 per month for a second person.

of costs will be covered for long-term care. Colonel Cook told us that a Fellowship Fund has been established to help those in financial distress.

In the lower level of the community building we saw an outstanding art exhibition of the Belfair Artists. Several of these Fairfax residents have achieved national recognition.

The Fairfax had a banner year in 1992: Marriott designated the Fairfax as their flagship community, the best of the eighteen communities they own and operate. The

CLIMATE—1991 TEMP. (°F), PRECIP. (IN.)					OF INTEREST—
	AVG.	MAX.	MIN.	PRECIP.	Total precipitation in 1991 was 29.64 inches. Snowfall ranges from about 16 to 37 inches a year.
JAN.	38.6	59	18	2.90	
APR.	58.2	87	35	1.39	
JULY	81.4	101	65	3.76	
OCT.	60.4	85	37	2.03	

health care center received top honors after ten days of inspection by state and federal agencies. The year ended with a 97 percent occupancy, and there is now a waiting list.

The Fairfax, 9140 Belvoir Woods Parkway, Fort Belvoir, VA 22060
703/799-1000

FUTURE

Falcons Landing, Sterling, Virginia

The Cascades is a three-thousand-acre master planned residential community with libraries, schools, day care centers, shopping, and recreational areas. It is located twenty miles northwest of Washington, D.C., along the Potomac River. Within the Cascades, Falcons Landing will be built on thirty-three acres. All that currently exists is an information center.

Falcons Landing will be a life-care community with 239 apartments in five connected buildings, 80 single-family and duplex homes, and a 45,000-square-foot community center. The health center will have a 60-bed nursing facility with 30 additional beds for assisted living.

Retired air force officers, retired officers from other uniformed services, and single officers' widows and widowers are eligible, as are special exceptions as approved; residents must be sixty-two years of age at time of occupancy. Opening is scheduled for fall of 1995.

Falcons Landing is owned by the Air Force Retired Officers Community–Washington (AFROC), a non-profit corporation organized in 1984 to develop and operate the community. The corporation suffered a severe setback in late 1990 when its builder and facility manager withdrew just as construction was about to begin. The Haskell Community Developers joined forces with AFROC and a new site was found. Construction should start in spring 1994.

We met with Marketing Director Bob Korman at the information center. Mr. Korman has been associated with Haskell since 1987 in a marketing and development capacity. Previously he was associated with Fleet Landing near Jacksonville, Florida, which was also developed by Haskell.

Falcons Landing, 20401 Falcons Landing Circle, Sterling, VA 20165
800/952-3762

RELIGIOUS

Many religious denominations sponsor RCs throughout the country. Of those we surveyed, we found three that offered an opportunity for in-depth spiritual growth and fulfillment during the retirement years.

ALEXIAN VILLAGE, SIGNAL MOUNTAIN, TENNESSEE

Life Care on Top of the Mountain

In the south central area of Tennessee, near the Georgia and Alabama borders, the Tennessee River winds around

Alexian Village offers majestic views of the Tennessee River valley.

mountains in a gigantic "U" configuration. Sometime around 1815 John Ross, a Cherokee Indian chief, established a ferry across the river in the vicinity of the "U." This was known as Ross's Landing, and later as Chattanooga.

In this same area during the Civil War, Union soldiers on Signal Mountain signaled their comrades across the river on Lookout Mountain. Today Alexian Village is atop Signal Mountain, and hang-glider enthusiasts fly off Lookout Mountain.

Centuries before any of these events, in 1334, the Religious Order of the Alexian Brothers was founded in Aachen, Germany. The order was named for St. Alexius, a Roman nobleman who gave up his wealth to work with the sick.

In 1938 the Alexian Brothers world headquarters moved from Germany to the present thirty-three-acre property on top of Signal Mountain, a 1912 building once known as the Signal Mountain Inn to a monastery.

In 1983 Alexian Village opened as a subsidiary of Alexian Brothers Health Systems, Inc., a National Catholic Health Care Corporation. After several additions, the village now has 360 apartments, of which 42 units opened in January 1993.

Also on-site is a 120-bed skilled nursing health care center. The original Signal Mountain Inn resort inn property has been completely renovated and is now an assisted living facility. The elegance of the former resort is evident in the expansive foyer styled in the manner of grand 1920s hotels: a fourteen-foot ceiling, two huge working fireplaces, aviary, aquarium, large-screen TV, and an abundance of conversation nooks.

The main building of the community has a promenade with many conversation alcoves, as well as a coffee shop, library and reading room, country store, mail boxes, meeting hall, game room, and bank. The dining room has a magnificent view of what is known as the Tennessee Grand Canyon and the Cumberland Plateau. The large, newly constructed chapel is down the hall from the dining room.

Also available is a sauna, Jacuzzi, heated swimming pool, exercise center, ceramics room with four kilns, and a well-equipped woodworking shop. Two vans and two limousines provide transportation for the entire community.

There is a minimum age of sixty-two; the average age is seventy-nine, and seventy-three at time of move-in. Residents come from all over the country, with about one third from Florida. Although most faiths are represented, about 30 percent of the residents are Roman Catholic.

There are two fees: a life use fee that is paid at the time of move-in, and a monthly service fee. Three cost examples follow:

UNIT	LIFE USE FEE	MONTHLY SERVICE FEE	
		Single Occupancy	Double Occupancy
Studio	$ 44,000	$ 757	N/A
2 bedrooms, 1½ baths	99,000	935	$1,385
2 bedrooms, 2 baths	124,000	1,257	1,669

The service fee covers one meal a day, bimonthly housekeeping service, flat linen service, and use of all community amenities and common areas. If a resident requires a move to assisted living, the monthly fee remains the same as that which was paid for the apartment. If one or both members of a couple requires a move to the health center, intermediate care, or skilled nursing care, the total monthly fee for husband and wife also remains the same as that which was paid for the apartment.

The village is at an elevation of 1,800 feet, 1,000 feet higher than the base of the mountain. The total population of Signal Mountain is about 8,000, with 1,500 residents living on the top. About three miles from the village is a large shopping area. Chattanooga, with an estimated population of 153,800 in 1992, is eight miles away along a curving road down the mountain.

We visited with residents Jack and Genie Henry in their prime-location apartment. They moved into the new building, which was built on the edge of the bluff, in January 1993. Their two-bedroom apartment with spacious living room has an unobstructed view of the gorge. They said that watching the early morning mist rising up from the valley and slowly dissipating in the sun is much better than watching the morning shows on TV.

The Henrys lived on Signal Mountain before their retirement, so their move was comparatively easy. Their newfound friends and activities in the village, along with their longtime friends in the area, keep them very busy. The availability of life care and freedom from keeping up a big house were their primary reasons for making the move. Jack is a member of the continuing education committee, and both are active in "downtown" activities.

During our survey of the community we crossed paths with a few of the Brothers, who always gave us a smile and cheery hello. We came away with a feeling that the values, ethics, and ideals of the Alexian Brothers permeate this life-care community in a quiet, sincere manner

CLIMATE—1991 TEMP. (°F), PRECIP. (IN.)				OF INTEREST—
	AVG.	MAX.	MIN.	PRECIP.	Statistics shown here are from the weather station at the base of the mountain.
JAN.	42.6	61	19	2.71	
APR.	63.7	83	37	6.78	
JULY	81.5	97	69	3.59	
OCT.	61.4	84	34	0.22	

that is comforting and reassuring—a wonderful environment for the later years.

Alexian Village, 100 James Blvd., Signal Mountain, TN 37377
800/251-4600

LAKE JUNALUSKA ASSEMBLY, LAKE JUNALUSKA, NORTH CAROLINA

United Methodist Southeastern Jurisdictional Conference Center

"It's a way of life," said Pat Maier, the first person we met at Junaluska.

"It's a way of life," Betsy Seymour agreed four days later when we surveyed the Carriage Club in Charlotte, North Carolina (see page 77) and mentioned to her that we had been to Junaluska.

Pat went on to say that she was fifteen years old

The chapel at Lake Junaluska sits on the shore of the community's 200-acre lake. (Photo by Dwight Herlong)

when she made her first trip to the Assembly, followed by many more summers of learning and fun. Both of her daughters have had the same experience. Ten years ago she bought a lot, built a home on it seven years later, and will become a full-time volunteer at the Assembly when she retires as a school librarian. During her summer break she is a volunteer receptionist in the public relations department.

The excitement and sincerity of these two ladies, and many other residents we talked with, led us to feel that living at Junaluska offers an opportunity for a satisfying later life.

Lake Junaluska is in Haywood County (population nearly 47,000) in the western part of North Carolina. It is located on 1,200 acres three miles from the county seat of Waynesville (population 8,000), and has a two-hundred-bed acute care hospital. Asheville, with a regional airport, is twenty-seven miles to the east. The terrain is heavily wooded and in the foothills of the Great Smoky Mountains. The Cataloochee Ski Area is nearby, as is I-40. Within twenty-five miles are three entrances to the Great Smoky Mountains National Park and four entrances to the Blue Ridge Parkway.

Lake Junaluska had its start in May 1900, when a group of leaders of the Methodist Episcopal Church South met to consider ways and means of deepening the missionary interests in their own church. The group formed a laymen's missionary movement that became a formal organization in 1908, and in 1913 resulted in the official opening of what is today Lake Junaluska Assembly.

The entire facility encircles a two hundred-acre lake. There are two entrances: the east gate entrance is dramatic, up a grade and around a curve. There is a large cross on a bluff that overlooks the $25 million complex. Around the lake are two hotels with a total of 235 rooms, lodges and apartments with 155 rooms, and private cottages and apartments that are rented on a weekly basis. On-site are dining and meeting rooms; Stuart Auditorium, which seats 2,500 people; an adult center; a children's ministry and youth center; a memorial chapel; a bookstore; and a post office. Golf and other sports activities are also available. Numerous other buildings house offices for the major functions of the Assembly.

Private homes dot the hillsides surrounding the lake. Some are new, and others were built many years ago. Tri-Vista Village, a fifty-six-condominium development, was built in the late 1980s. Lots are sold on a limited basis each year. Lake Junaluska Realty handles property sales. Following is a sampling of their listings from mid-1993:

Privately owned lot, Kilgore Road	$11,500
Tri-Vista Villas—Lower level, 2 bedrooms, 2 baths	$74,900
Upper level	$79,900
Custom log home, 2,165 sq. ft. finished area, 4 bedrooms, 3 baths; basement has 1,225 sq. ft., unfinished but wired and plumbed for finished apartment, .63-acre lot	
total cost	$127,500

Approximately 600 families own homes and 350 live there year-round. Of these, nearly all are retirees. Homeowners can buy a yearly pass for $100 that entitles them to the use of all facilities. Land has been sold to a for-profit group to build a retirement community with adjacent health care housing 250 residents in apartments and villas. Construction is expected to begin sometime in 1994. The Assembly will provide use of its facilities for exercise and sports activities.

The 1993 calendar included 168 individual events with the theme "Catching God's Vision." Programs, which varied from one day to a week, featured fifteen Elderhostel trips, a lay witness celebration, five mid-winter youth retreats, a choir/music weekend, a growing-in-marriage retreat, Seventh Day Adventists camp meeting, white-water adventure trip, United Methodist ministers' conference, conference of older adult ministry, Thanksgiving and Christmas at Junaluska, many concerts by the Junaluska Singers, and more.

The July 8, 1993, issue of *The Assembly Daily* listed such activities as the Junaluska flea market and barbecue, adult center news, laymen's breakfast, and a reminder to volunteer ushers concerning Sunday morning worship at Stuart Auditorium. Junaluska residents say they rarely need to think, "Wonder what I'll do today?"

The 1,200 acres have been developed gradually over eighty years. As money was raised, new facilities were built. Neat, clean, and functional best describe the community. After walking around the community, seeing smiling faces, and hearing friendly hellos, we understand their axiom, "There's something about coming home to Junaluska."

CLIMATE—1991 TEMP. (°F), PRECIP. (IN.)   OF INTEREST—

	AVG.	MAX.	MIN.	PRECIP.	
JAN.	39.2	63	13	3.25	Total precipitation in 1991 was 43.66 inches. Annual precipitation ranges from 27 to 65 inches. Snowfall in 1991 was 3.5 inches.
APR.	58.4	82	33	5.38	
JULY	75.2	91	59	6.07	
OCT.	57.0	80	30	0.19	

Lake Junaluska Assembly, P.O. Box 67, Lake Junaluska, NC 28745
704/452-2881   800/222-4930

SEACREST VILLAGE, ENCINITAS, CALIFORNIA

Senior Living in the Jewish Tradition

In the coastal city of Encinitas in southern California, a short distance off I-5, is Seacrest Village, which opened in 1989. The entryway has a great view of the Pacific Ocean.

The main building is the Garden Court, a two-story, ninety-eight-unit residential apartment complex that encloses a large, beautifully landscaped courtyard. On the first floor are apartments, a spacious lobby, administrative offices, a mail room, hair salon, gift shop, sidewalk café, arts and crafts room, and library. The second floor has more apartments, along with dining facilities, a living room, theater room, clinic, and synagogue. A fifty-eight-bed medical center adjoins the Garden Court on this ten-acre plot.

The Village is a development of the San Diego Hebrew Home, a non-profit organization that has provided care to the Jewish community for forty-five years. It is a completely kosher facility; eight hundred place settings of dishes, silverware, glasses, and so on are used to maintain the laws of kashrut that require separate dishes for meat and dairy meals and on Passover.

Robin Israel, director of marketing, explained the in-

The Garden Court at Seacrest Village is a residential complex that surrounds a large courtyard.

tricacies of admission to Seacrest Village. Potential Village residents must live in San Diego County or have children who have lived in the county for at least five years. About 70 percent of the current residents are from San Diego and 30 percent from out of state. Ages range from seventy to ninety-nine, with an average age of eighty-three. Ten of the ninety-eight apartments are occupied by couples.

This is a rental community with no up-front payment. Three meals are served daily. There are studio, one-bedroom, and larger one-bedroom deluxe apartments.

Rents range from $1,375 to $2,350 per month with a $400 charge for the second person. Once admitted, no one has ever been asked to leave for financial reasons.

Many residents do volunteer work in the medical center, library, gift shop, front desk, home care agency, and special projects within the Village.

Robin mentioned a continuing problem concerning seating arrangements during meals: the "old guard" likes to sit at "their table." This makes it difficult for the newcomer. We have heard of similar problems at many other communities. She told us, however, that there is a deep bonding among the residents. Some are from Russia, and many lost family members during the Holocaust. The Jewish tradition, philosophy, and commitment live on.

This camaraderie was evident at the Sidewalk Café just off of the lobby, where we enjoyed a cup of coffee from the community pot. Residents were cheerful and talkative as they waited for the mid-morning cookies to be brought out from the kitchen. A woman who called herself "Rose from Chicago" joked about the way she

CLIMATE—1991 TEMP. (°F), PRECIP. (IN.)				OF INTEREST—
AVG.	MAX.	MIN.	PRECIP.	85 percent of rainfall occurs November through March. In 1991, total precipitation was 13.51 inches. The highest temperatures occur in September and October. Snow is rare.
JAN. 57.4	79	42	1.06	
APR. 61.7	80	51	0.05	
JULY 67.4	76	60	0.24	
OCT. 68.0	92	48	0.69	

always succumbed to the cookie plate, although she knew she shouldn't. This jovial lady, with a positive attitude about life, caused us to reflect on the benefits of retirement living in the Jewish tradition.

Seacrest Village, 211 Saxony Rd., Encinitas, CA 92024
619/632-0081

FUTURE

Covenant Village of Colorado, Westminster, Colorado

We have visited many of the twelve Covenant Villages that are home to more than 3,600 senior adults in the United States. Our impression is that they are all first-class communities.

The villages are part of the ministry of the Evangelical Covenant Church, with more than 106 years of experience in serving seniors.

The Colorado village, a 280-unit continuing-care facility in the Denver suburb of Westminster, will be built on twenty-four acres. It is designed for adults at least sixty-two years of age, and will have a sixty-room assisted-living complex as well as a sixty-bed nursing center. There will be an entrance fee and monthly fee.

According to a brochure that contains the Covenant retirement community's mission statement, "spiritual growth will be met by encouraging Christian fellowship, chapel services, classes, seminars, and Bible studies, should they [the residents] so choose."

Covenant Village of Colorado, 9153 Ammons St., Westminster, CO 80021
303/424-4828
Covenant Retirement Communities, 5115 North Francisco Ave., Suite 200, Chicago, IL 60625
312/878-2294

COLLEGIATE

The number of RCs on or adjacent to a college or university campus is increasing dramatically. These communities offer a unique opportunity for a lifetime of learning along with the other benefits of RC living.

COLLEGE LANDINGS/COLLEGE HARBOR, ST. PETERSBURG, FLORIDA

Age-Progressive Learning, Giving, and Living

The feature picture on a brochure for Eckerd College Academy of Senior Professionals (ASPEC) is the touchdown of an open-cockpit ultralight aircraft, *The Spirit of ASPEC*. At the controls and waving to the photographer is Art Peterson, director of ASPEC. In the copy accompanying an insert picture of the gray-haired director, he describes the joy he and four other ASPEC members experienced as they spent two years building the aircraft.

The risk-taking endeavor is symbolic of the progressive direction Eckerd College has taken in bringing together students, faculty, and senior professionals in a unique learning environment.

This liberal arts college, founded as Florida Presbyterian College in 1958, is related by covenant to the Presbyterian Church (USA). The sixty-six modern air-conditioned buildings are on 267 acres of property overlooking Boca Ciega Bay in St. Petersburg, Florida. The college is located off Pinellas Bayway, leading to the gulf beaches and the greater bay area communities of Tampa, Clearwater, Sarasota, and Bradenton. Access to I-275 is nearby.

The "homemade aircraft" picture brochure explains what the Senior Professional program is all about. The founding principle behind ASPEC is "to provide an intellectually stimulating environment for retired professionals and high achievers—a place where the wealth of experience could be shared with like-minded individuals and the college community."

The 1,350-member student body is diverse, coming from forty-eight states and fifty-two foreign countries. There are eighty-four full-time faculty with an average age of forty-two. This equates to a fourteen-to-one student-faculty ratio. Eckerd has a complete program of intercollegiate and intramural athletics for men and women, and an award-winning waterfront program (including a marina safety and rescue team). It is a member of the NCAA (Division II) and the Sunshine State Conference. Awards and credits are impressive.

Included in the 1993 membership roster are short biographies of the 181 members. Diversity is evident: entrepreneurs, attorneys, professors (from the United States and abroad), corporate officers, medical doctors, and authors, including Pulitzer Prize winner James A. Michener.

Members have many options, including lectures, forums, and discussion colloquia; monthly luncheons; interest groups; individual research, writing, study, or service (funded independently or by external grants); informal discussions with colleagues, faculty, and students; or specialized instructional assistance at the invitation of college faculty. Lewis House, the six-thousand-square-foot ASPEC meeting building, is a beehive of activities that vary from structured programs to brown-bag lunches.

The latest innovative venture of the college is the building of College Landings, an age-restricted community, on campus property. This is a townhouse and villa project overlooking Boca Ciega Bay and within walking distance of Lewis House. Residents must be fifty-five and over, with no minor children. This will be a gated community with gazebos, courts, greenways, and gaslights along the streets. The townhouses will have a garage on the first level with living space on the second level, and will be built in interconnecting groups of two, three, and four units.

Villa lots range from $199,000 for those fronting the bay to $95,000 for those fronting on a manmade lake. Townhomes, including homesite, range from a 2 bedroom/2 bath, 1,164 square feet for $132,000, to a 2 or 3 bedroom/2 bath/family room, 2,000 square feet at

$191,000. The monthly fee is $164. Land development had begun when we were there in April 1993. Build-out is expected in five years.

Adjacent to College Landings is College Harbor, an apartment retirement community with health care. This also faces the bay. Five apartment sizes are available, from an alcove (500 square feet) to a three-bedroom apartment (1,675 square feet).

Three cost packages are available: (1) a lease program, (2) endowment and monthly fee with some health care, and (3) a bond purchase larger than the cost of #2 but with a 100 percent refund, monthly fee, and some health care. These plans include all utilities, one meal a day, housekeeping services, transportation, and use of the amenities.

Medical care, from assisted living to skilled nursing, is available in the medical center. Over the years we have surveyed College Harbor three times and have always found the residents enthusiastic about the community.

Many people move from place to place during their retirement years. Unfortunately this requires starting over in a new environment and leaving friends behind each time a move is made. Medical requirements often influence these decisions as aging takes its toll.

Eckerd College presents an interesting alternative. Upon retirement, residents purchase a low maintenance villa or townhouse at College Landings in sunny Florida and get involved in ASPEC activities with their spouse. As they age, if they decide it would be easier to live where more services are available, they can move to Col-

CLIMATE—1991 TEMP. (°F), PRECIP. (IN.)				OF INTEREST—
	AVG.	MAX.	MIN.	PRECIP.
JAN.	66.7	86	40	2.41
APR.	76.8	92	50	1.54
JULY	82.3	95	70	9.92
OCT.	75.3	90	51	0.78

OF INTEREST— Total precipitation in 1991 was 43.16 inches. Freezing temperatures occur one or two mornings a year.

lege Harbor without disrupting the friendships they've established within the academic community, ASPEC, and College Landings. Medical services, including assisted living, are available as needed, allowing friendships, old and new, to continue. And when the inevitable happens, the survivor is still in a supportive environment among friends made over the years.

After retirement, it's still possible to make contributions to others, continue learning, bask in the glow of friendships, and say to ourselves, "well done." An invigorating, progressive college campus like Eckerd could make this happen.

ASPEC/Eckerd College, 4200 54th Ave. So., St. Petersburg, FL 33711
813/864-8834
College Landings, 4500 Pinellas Bayway, St. Petersburg, FL 33711
813/864-9300
College Harbor, 4600 54th Ave. So., St. Petersburg, FL 33711
813/866-3124

THE COLONNADES, CHARLOTTESVILLE, VIRGINIA

U.S. History Buff's Utopia

When the "Sage of Monticello," Thomas Jefferson, founded the University of Virginia (UVA), he also designed the campus, supervised construction and the hiring of the faculty. More than two hundred years later The Colonnades was built on fifty-seven acres of UVA Real Estate Foundation property. The community was sponsored by the UVA Alumni Association, Real Estate Foundation, and the Health Sciences Foundation.

Architecturally, the complex has a distinct UVA flavor: red brick buildings with white columns, and a main building with a dome. Marriott Corporation built and manages the complex. Ninety-nine years from the date of its opening in September 1991, The Colonnades in its entirety will belong to the university. There are 217 units, of which 170 are occupied. The average age is seventy-five.

We inquired about interaction between the community and the university and received a two-page list of activities that included: weekly transportation to the campus for those doing research; bimonthly lecture series at UVA Center on Aging and Health; monthly Rotunda tours during the academic year; lectures given at The Colonnades by speakers from the Department of Ophthalmology, Center for Russian and East European Studies, Depart-

The Main Pavillion at The Colonnades mirrors the southern architectual flavor of its residential buildings—red brick with white trim and columns.
(PHOTO BY MOLLY BASS)

ment of Spanish, Italian and Portuguese; Department of History, and Political and Social Thought Program; UVA plays and musicals; Bayly Art Museum monthly trips; Miller Center lectures; a Colonnades Cup Polo Match; participation in two research studies in the School of Education; and continuing education courses at The Colonnades.

Not all activities at The Colonnades center on UVA, however. The monthly recreation calendar includes a jewelry workshop, needleworkers/knitting workshop, painting studio, bookmobile, sing-along, bridge groups, music lovers club, women's club, investment club, exercise classes, social hour each Wednesday afternoon, Saturday night movies, and Vespers each Sunday evening. Included on-site are a bank, indoor swimming pool, health club, woodworking shop, country store, garden plots, and natural walking paths.

Charlottesville is in the center of the state, 70 miles from Richmond, 110 miles from Washington, D.C. It is a small (population 42,900) rural college community with mild winters. The town has its own identity; it is not a bedroom community to a large city. In 1989 University Hospital opened on the UVA campus. Two faculty members—Dr. Diane Snystad, an internist, and Dr. Richard Lindsay, head of geriatrics—share on-call duties at the Colonnades clinic.

East-west Interstate 64 touches the southern edge of the town, and the Blue Ridge Parkway is twenty miles east. The Charlottesville-Albemarle Airport is served by four airlines.

Six apartment and two cottage styles are available. A cost example, for 2 bedrooms/2 baths:

	STANDARD ENDOWMENT 90% Refundable		
	Entry	Monthly	Monthly Rental
Apartment	$151,725–159,600	$1,250	—
Cottage	209,750–216,575	1,500	—
Second person add	6,300	315	

	MODIFIED ENDOWMENT 90% Refundable		
	Entry	Monthly	Monthly Rental
Apartment	$ 75,900–79,800	$1,800	$2,200–2,595
Cottage	104,875–108,300	2,215	2,700–3,060
Second person add	4,200	420	525

Services include thirty meals a month; weekly housekeeping; flat linen service; utilities (except telephone); exterior/interior maintenance; scheduled transportation; social, cultural, and educational activities; and routine medical care at the on-site clinic. Assisted living and nursing care are available at additional cost.

We met with resident Edwina (Dee) Pancake, who belongs to the Pioneer Club (the seven residents who moved in the very first day), and Frank Jobes, board chairman of the residents association. Dee serves on the service and security, and communications committees. She laughingly remarked, "I feel like a den mother to the communication committee." She is an active volunteer with Recordings for the Blind and Hospice. Frank chaired the association by-laws committee and wrote the charters for nearly every committee.

Both residents stressed the importance of the Marriott Residents' Satisfaction Survey, conducted every six months at all thirteen Marriott communities. According to the personal feedback the survey collects, Frank said, "The general satisfaction of The Colonnades is high." The association is working with Marriott to increase the size of the common room and library. From what we observed, it appears there is a great deal of openness between the board and the administration.

While we were touring the facility with Sarah Odom, activities director, a resident asked Sarah, "Are you showing these people around? I know they're going to like it." Sarah told her about our book and the resident said, "This certainly should be number one."

We have not given ratings to any community, but felt this facility and its unique tie-in with UVA warranted inclusion in the book.

CLIMATE—1991 TEMP. (°F), PRECIP. (IN.)   OF INTEREST—

	AVG.	MAX.	MIN.	PRECIP.	
JAN.	38.9	65	12	3.00	Total precipitation in 1991 was 34.47 inches. The community is on the eastern edge of the Blue Ridge Mountains. Snowfall in 1991 was 18.3 inches.
APR.	57.8	85	31	2.80	
JULY	78.5	96	63	4.51	
OCT.	59.6	87	33	0.62	

The Colonnades, 2600 Barracks Rd., Charlottesville, VA 22901
804/971-1892

THE FOREST AT DUKE, DURHAM, NORTH CAROLINA

A Dream Come True

Duke University is a forerunner in offering a wide selection of courses to active retirees. For example: Great Decisions 1993, Struggling Couples on Screen, Parapsychology, 20th Century Christian Theologians, Jewish Cultures of the Past and Present, Creative Writing, Irish Studies, Secret Language of Music, Journalists Roundtable, and Comedy Restored. These are just a few of the courses offered by the Duke Institute for Learning in Retirement (DILR), which celebrated its sixteenth year in 1993. The winter 1993 catalog included twenty pages of noncredit courses. Each class is held one day a week for one-and-one-half hours from January 11 to March 22. All classes except swimming are held in the Bishop's House on the East Campus.

A full membership costs $110 and entitles a resident to enroll in up to five classes per semester. The DILR is a self-governing group within the limits of Duke policies. Each member has voting privileges and may hold an office. In addition to the classes, DILR offers a variety of activities and social events, including bridge groups, a chamber music group, dine-outs, dinner theater, potluck dinners, and parties. Membership also provides access to the libraries, use of swimming pools during free-swim

The community center at The Forest at Duke is flanked by apartment buildings.

hours, language labs, East Campus faculty dining room, and course-audit privileges at 10 percent of the university course fee.

One highlight of the Duke campus is the Duke Chapel, a dramatic Gothic structure that recalls European splendor with seventy-seven stained glass windows, a 210-foot bell tower, and a fifty-bell carillon.

DILR's stimulating learning program, coupled with the very full activity calendar at The Forest, gives residents many ways to live their life to the fullest.

We have followed the development of The Forest since 1989; our first on-site survey was in May 1992. The excellent location, partially completed buildings, and proximity to Duke University dictated that we must make a return trip.

We weren't disappointed when we drove into the forty-two-acre community and conducted our survey. The Forest is in a suburban area south of downtown Durham, very close to Business 15-501, which makes it easy to reach any place in Durham. I-85 and I-40 provide convenient access to other cities in the Raleigh-Durham–Chapel Hill triangle. The Raleigh-Durham International Airport is thirteen miles away.

Durham's population in 1992 was nearly 182,000, an increase of 35.1 percent from 1980. It is referred to as the City of Medicine: the leading industry is medicine, with more than 25 percent of the total workforce employed in health-related fields.

The Forest is a non-profit continuing-care retirement community that opened for occupancy on September 1, 1992. Eighty percent of the units are occupied and 95 percent are reserved. One resident in each household must be sixty-five or older. The average resident age is seventy-six.

The community includes 161 apartments and 80 duplex cottages. The terrain is sloping, so some apartment buildings are three stories in front and four stories in the back. All apartment buildings are connected to the community center, outpatient clinic, and health care center. Cottages flank the central area, in cul-de-sac layouts along the curving roadway that encircles the complex. There are two nongated entryways.

There are five sizes of apartments and three sizes of cottages, and there are three entry-fee refund plans: (1) refund amortized over fifty months, (2) 50 percent refunded after fifty months, and (3) 100 percent refund when leaving the community. Examples:

2-bedroom apartment, 1,144 sq. ft., double occupancy
  Entry fee (1) $136,000 (2) $176,080 (3) $225,940
  Monthly service fee $1,925
2-bedroom cottage, 1,445 sq. ft., double occupancy
  Entry fee (1) $161,390 (2) $208,690 (3) $268,790
  Monthly service fee $2,031

Each resident is entitled to ten days a year in the health care center at no extra charge. According to the Residence and Care Agreement, a single resident who moves permanently to the health care center will pay 40 percent of the daily rate for the health care center instead of the monthly service fee. For a married couple, the double-occupancy monthly fee will remain in effect if one spouse moves permanently to the health care center, and the only additional payment would be 15 percent of the daily rate in the nursing center.

Amenities and services included in the monthly fee are use of the auditorium, formal dining room, café, bank, beauty/barber shop, gift shop, library, craft/art studio, indoor pool, exercise room, woodworking shop, billiards, card room, garden plots, and classroom; plus one meal daily, all utilities except telephone, emergency call and response, scheduled transportation, twenty-four-hour security, continuing education programs, and recreational programs.

The life-care program includes an exercise wellness

program, routine physician care, rehabilitative services, routine laboratory and diagnostic tests, visiting nurse assistance in living units, and assistance with filing insurance claims.

We were guests of Nelson and DeEtte Strawbridge for morning coffee at their cottage. DeEtte said she resisted a move to The Forest for three years. Her reason was that they lived in a seven thousand-square-foot house on a golf course, and she wasn't ready for community living. But eight months after making the move, she said, "It's like an extended vacation—I haven't been this relaxed in a long time."

Nelson, the president of the residents association, told us about some issues that were under discussion at the time, such as a recent 6-percent service fee increase to maintain the reserve fund and keep the sixty-bed health center operating. Nelson also mentioned a reorganization of the community management team, which was less than a year old, and a debate among residents over whether to have all of the common grounds landscaped and manicured (some felt most areas should be left in their natural state, including the poison ivy!).

In 1980, sixty university faculty, staff, and neighbors acquired thirty-five acres of land on Pickett Road adjacent to their homes. A tremendous need became evident throughout Durham for an RC that could take advantage of the many opportunities offered by Duke University.

Dr. James D. Crapo took the lead and visited dozens of RCs throughout the United States. A first-class, not-

CLIMATE—1991 TEMP. (°F), PRECIP. (IN.)

	AVG.	MAX.	MIN.	PRECIP.
JAN.	41.9	66	19	4.12
APR.	62.3	86	36	1.04
JULY	80.6	96	67	10.27
OCT.	61.1	84	35	1.40

OF INTEREST—
Total precipitation in 1991 was 34.46 inches. Only a trace of snow fell in 1990–91, but 1988–89 had 12 inches. Some snow and/or sleet usually occurs each year.

for-profit dream of a continuing-care retirement community emerged. The dream came true.

The Forest at Duke, 2701 Pickett Rd., Durham, NC 27705
919/490-8000

FUTURE

The Kendal Corporation is a non-profit organization serving older people. The directors are members of the Religious Society of Friends (Quakers). The first Kendal community, Kendal at Longwood, Kennett Square, Pennsylvania, opened in 1973, is still operating, and has an AAHA Continuing Care accreditation. Their "Values and Standards" brochure is a comprehensive statement of their beliefs and method of operation. We observed this in action when, years ago, we surveyed Pennswood

Village in Newtown, Pennsylvania, and have no concern whatsoever in endorsing these two future developments.

Kendal at Oberlin, Oberlin, Ohio

Thirty-five miles southwest of Cleveland is the small town of Oberlin, home of Oberlin College (founded in 1833) and its renowned Conservatory of Music. A plaque on Tappen Square reads, OBERLIN DOWNTOWN 1833. Facing the square is a Ben Franklin five-and-ten store in a turn-of-the-century building.

Less than a mile down tree-lined streets is the ninety-two-acre continuing-care retirement community. The buildings opened in December 1993.

Kendal at Oberlin, P.O. Box 519, Oberlin, OH 44074
216/775-0094

Kendal at Ithaca, Ithaca, New York

This planned continuing-care community in the Finger Lakes Region of New York, located near Cornell University, is projected to open in 1995.

The Kendal Corporation, Kennett Square, PA 19348
215/338-7001

HAVE A GREAT RETIREMENT

Our thumbnail description of retirement is:

1. *Changes*—Retirement causes a chain reaction of changes. The more you plan, the easier the changes will be.
2. *Choices*—Many lifestyle choices and options emerge.
3. *Opportunities*—Retirement happiness is readily available. A positive attitude and a determination to live the rest of your life to the fullest is a must.

The "50 Best" listing will serve as a foundation for further investigation of RC lifestyles. Before hitting the road, obtain a current brochure from the RCs that interest you. It's also a good idea to request a newcomer information packet from the local chamber of commerce.

Analyze the information, then put together a tour of

RCs. If possible, take advantage of vacation packages or inquire about the use of a guest room on-site.

Once you arrive, don't be bashful. Ask as many probing questions as you can think of when talking with the staff, residents association officers, and resident assigned as your host. Find ways to engage other residents in conversation by rambling around on your own. Discuss your concerns. Most likely those who have made the move had similar concerns, and listening to their experiences will be very helpful.

Ask for an annual report, disclosure statement, and names and details about the board of directors. Check your local library to obtain a Dun & Bradstreet report on the "for profit" communities. Of extreme importance is the degree to which the residents association is involved. Is it cosmetic, or do they really know what's going on?

During discussions, ask who, what, when, where, how, how much, and why. Follow up on the replies with "Could you expand on that a bit more?" A well-run RC administration will not be offended by in-depth probing. They will welcome your interest, because they know that a satisfied resident is their best marketing representative.

After the trip and the accumulation of all material, it's discussion and decision time. If you're making plans with a partner, a joint decision, not a decision by edict, is critically important. If necessary, make a second or third trip to the places you like most before you decide. Relocation and starting anew are not to be taken lightly.

Our twofold purpose has been:

1. To provide our readers with a look inside the 50 best retirement communities in America.

   We included layout, services, amenities, costs, and other information, but most important we wanted to convey the ambiance and the pulse of the community. We included a wide diversity of RCs with a geographical spread across the United States, and pricing from affordable to upper middle income.

2. To answer the question, What are RCs all about? The ten chapters answer this question as best we can.

Writing this book has been an exciting experience. Our research stretched from the Atlantic to the Pacific and from San Antonio, Texas, to Minneapolis, Minnesota. In 1993 we were on the road for a total of thirteen weeks: 10,175 air miles, 6,825 miles on rental cars, and 5,985 miles on our personal car, traveling through twenty-eight states.

Each person we talked to—and there were hundreds—made us feel a part of their community. We made a host of new acquaintances. Unfortunately, we know that our paths probably will never cross again. There may be one exception—we are giving serious consideration to a move to one of our "50 best" choices.

Every day was a learning experience and gave us a personal sense of achievement. It was fun researching and writing this book. We sincerely hope it will be helpful to preretirees and retirees who are looking forward to an active, productive retirement.

HAVE A GREAT RETIREMENT!

index

ALPHABETICAL

BY STATE

BY CLASSIFICATION